TRON *theatre*

co-production

WORLD STAGE PREMIERE

sea urchins

by Sharman Macdonald

Sea Urchins

plays at the Dundee Rep Theatre from
Wednesday 20 May to Saturday 6 June
and at the Tron Theatre from
Wednesday 17 June to Saturday 11 July 1998

Cover photo: Carol Gordon

Tron Theatre Limited

63 Trongate, Glasgow G1 5HB
Box Office   0141 552 4267
Administration   0141 552 3748
Bars/Restaurant   0141 552 8587
Fax   0141 552 6657
Web   www.tron.co.uk

Dundee Rep Theatre

Tay Square, Dundee DD1 1PB
Box Office   01382 223530
Administration   01382 227684
Het Theatercafé   01382 206699
Fax   01382 228609
Community   01382 224877 or 223963
Scottish Dance Theatre   01382 229500

sea urchins

by Sharman Macdonald

The Williams Family – on holiday in Wales from Scotland

JOHN	Gilly Gilchrist
AILSA	Alison Peebles
RENA	Jenny Eddie ⎫
	Natasha Gray ⎭ (Dundee)
	Kimberley Gallacher ⎫
	Judith McCartney ⎭ (Glasgow)

The Williams Family – Wales

DAVID	David Royle
DORA	Maxine Evans
GARETH	Patrick Taggart
RHIANNON	Siobhan Flynn
NOELLE	Rachel Hendry ⎫
	Emma Ruthven Hughes ⎭ (Dundee)
	Claire Joss (Glasgow)
MARTIN	Andrew Eddie ⎫
	Neil Walls ⎭ (Dundee)
	David Farmer (Glasgow)
MAN	Desmond Hamilton

Director	Irina Brown
Designer	Jacqueline Gunn
Lighting Design	Davy Cunningham
Musical Director and Sound Design	John Irvine
Dialect Coach	Ros Steen
Assistant Directors	Maxine Evans
	Desmond Hamilton
ASM on the Book	Viktoria Begg

The play is set on a coved, pebbled beach below a cliff near David's home on the Atlantic coast of Wales in 1961

Biographies

Jenny Eddie (Rena)

Jenny is in her final year at Kinloch Primary School Carnoustie. She has been a member of Carnoustie Theatre Club since she was seven and has appeared in various productions, most notably as Gretel in the 1996 pantomime production of *Hansel and Gretel*. More recently she was in the production of *Them and Us* which won the SCDA Angus Youth Trophy. She has also appeared in *Half a Sixpence* with the Arbroath Musical Society and *The Hunchback of Notre Dame* with Midas. Her hobbies include swimming and football.

Andrew Eddie (Martin)

Thirteen-year-old Andrew is involved with two local theatre groups – Carnoustie Theatre Club and Arbroath Theatre Club – and has performed in three pantomimes and various plays. At Perth Rep he has been involved in two professional productions – *The Sound of Music* and *As You Like It*. Andrew recently auditioned for the National Youth Music Theatre and got past the first round in Edinburgh, enabling him to take part in auditions in London. This is Andrew's first involvement with Dundee Rep and the Tron Theatre.

Maxine Evans (Dora)

Maxine's theatre work includes *Break, My Heart* (Sherman Theatre/HTV Wales), *Blood Libel* (Norwich Playhouse), *See How They Run, Thark* and *Tom Jones* (Newbury), *The Rivals, Dracula, Richard III, Chorus of Disapproval* and *Henry VI* (all York). Her television work includes *Departures, Mortimer's Law, Next of Kin, The Bill, Crimewatch, London's Burning* and *Public Eye*.

Siobhan Flynn (Rhiannon)

Siobhan trained at Lamda graduating in 1995. Her theatre work includes *Flying Blind, Our Day Out, That Was Wonderful Darling* and *Red Devils Trilogy* (Sherman Theatre), *Dido and Aeneas* (Welsh National Opera) and *Return Ticket to Christmas* (Pauper's Carnival). On television Siobhan has been seen on *Casualty, Flying Blind, Tales from the Crypt, The Girl*, Dennis Potter's *Karaoke, Justin Perfect, Better Days, Y Cloc, Bowen and Bowen* and *Everyman*. Her film work includes *Age of the Romantics* for Working Title Films and on radio *Cadfael* (BBC).

Kimberley Gallacher (Rena)

Kimberley has appeared in *Wee MacGreegor* and *Beauty and the Beast* at the Old Athenaeum (Scottish Youth Theatre), *Annie* at the Kings Theatre (Apollo Players) and played the Artful Dodger in a school production of *Oliver*. Kimberley attends Hutchesons' Grammar School.

Gilly Gilchrist (John)

Before training at the Bristol Old Vic Theatre School Gilly trained as a circus performer in Edinburgh. His theatre work includes *A Doll's House* (Young Vic), *Hamlet* (Almeida Theatre and Footsbarn Theatre), *Six Productions* (Guizer Theatre Co), *His Master's Voice* (Wildcat), *East* (TAG), *Little Red Riding Hood* (Cumbernauld Theatre), *The House with the Green Shutters* and *Desire* (Communicado Theatre), *Romeo and Juliet* (Brunton Theatre). Gilly's numerous television appearances include the recent *Looking After Jo Jo* and *The Knock*. He has also appeared in *Between the Lines*, *Minder*, *Taggart*, *The Hawk*, *Casualty* and *The Bill* as well as the films *The Investigator*, *Rob Roy*, *Comfort and Joy* and *Robin Hood*. On radio Gilly was in the BBC's *The Road to Vichy*.

Natasha Gray (Rena)

Twelve-year-old Natasha attends Braeview Academy in Dundee. It was Natasha's Mum Sharon and her Dad Scott who encouraged her to act and both are very supportive. For two years Natasha was a member of Theatre 2000 and performed in *Aladdin*, *The Dragon* and many other productions. She is currently a member of the National Youth Music Theatre and in 1996 took part in the Whitehall Theatre's Summer School and their production *Summer '96*. Natasha also recently performed as a backing singer at the Whitehall Theatre for the group Voulez Vous. At Dundee Rep Theatre Natasha was the Mayor of Munchkinland in their production of *The Wizard of Oz*.

David Farmer (Martin)

Thirteen-year-old Martin was born in Glasgow but lived in Baltimore until the age of ten. He has been an active member of the drama group at Hillhead High School for the past two years. He became interested in acting while studying Shakespeare plays at school. David's interests include playing blues and classical guitar, reading, ice hockey, baseball, basketball, tennis and socialising with his friends.

Desmond Hamilton (Man)

Desmond studied at the Royal Scottish Academy of Music and Drama. His theatre credits include *Spring Awakening* (Mercat), *The Cherry Orchard* (Chandler), *Stricken* (Old Athenaeum), *Agamemnon* (Warsaw Palace of Culture), *Tartuffe* and *Coriolanus* (New Athenaeum). On television Desmond has appeared in *Bad Boys* and *Born Kicking* (BBC) and *Cracker* (Granada). His film work includes *Love Potion* (BFI).

Rachel Hendry (Noelle)

Twelve-year-old Rachel is a first year pupil at St John's High School, Dundee. Her theatre work includes a Munchkin, Ozzian and Winkie in *The Wizard of Oz* (Dundee Rep Theatre, 1996/97), a club singer in *Bugsy Malone* (Ferryport Theatre Co, Gardyne Theatre, 1997), *The Fifteen Streets* (Secret Theatre, Dundee Rep Community Theatre, 1998). Rachel is a member of Dundee Rep Theatre's Junior Youth Theatre and is a keen piano and violin player.

Emma Ruthven Hughes (Noelle)

Twelve-year-old Emma is a pupil at Park Place Primary School, Dundee. Her theatre work includes numerous school plays, including two performances at the Bonar Hall. Emma is a keen viola player and a member of the Dundee Schools Training Orchestra. She is also a member of the Dundee Junior Schools Choir and has performed solo in the Caird Hall. Emma's other interests include rugby (she played with the Dundee Juniors for five years), going to Tannadice to watch Dundee United play football, rollerblading, reading, looking after her cat Malcolm and arts and crafts.

Claire Joss (Noelle)

Claire attends drama classes at Hillhead High School and has appeared in *Cinderella, Goosey Goosey Glasgow, Aladdin* (Pavilion), *Dick Whittington, Seven Brides for Seven Brothers* and *Annie* (Kings Theatre). She has attended the Christine Hinshelwood School of Dancing from the age of two and has certificates in Tap, Ballet, Modern Dance, Disco and Majorette. Claire's ambition is to take a degree in Music and Drama.

Judith McCartney (Rena)

Sea Urchins is Judith's first stage production. She has previously performed with her drama club, the Centre Stage Theatre Company. Judith attends St Aloysius school.

Alison Peebles (Ailsa)

Alison trained at Edinburgh College of Art. Her numerous theatre performances include *Shining Souls* (Old Vic), *Albertine in Five Times* (Clyde Unity), *Blood*

Wedding (Northern Stage), *Shining Souls* and *Inez De Castro* (Traverse Theatre), *Crimes of the Heart* (Manchester Royal Exchange), *Death and the Maiden* (Dundee Rep/Lyceum), *Sacred Hearts, Blood Wedding* and *Carmen* (Communicado), *Evil Doers* (The Bush Theatre), *Macbeth* (Tron Theatre), *Good Person of Setzuan* and *Peer Gynt* (Royal National Theatre). On televison Alison has appeared in *Rose, Bumping the Odds, The Final Cut, Taggart, Rab C Nesbitt, Strathblair, Casualty, The Advocates, Albert and the Lion, Miles is Better* and *Inez de Castro*. Her film work includes *The Acid House Trilogy, Braveheart, Mirror/Mirror, The Star* and *Witches*. Alison has also done extensive work in drama and features for BBC Radio 4, BBC Radio Scotland, the World Service and Radio 2. She has directed productions at the Royal Lyceum Theatre, Queen Margaret College and for Communicado Theatre Company where she is an Associate Director.

David Royle (David)

David trained at the Drama Centre, London graduating in 1993. His theatre work includes *Leaving* (Finborough Theatre), *Life is a Dream* (Arts Threshold) and *The Best Warm Beer in Brooklyn* (Kings Head). On television David has appearerd in *Dalziel and Pascoe, Cold Lazarus, Garath Cheeseman, Soldier Soldier, London's Burning, Hitler the Final Report* and *The Knock*.

Patrick Taggart (Gareth)

Patrick trained at the Welsh College of Music and Drama. His theatre work includes *Under the*

Bed and *Macbeth* (Sherman Theatre), *Tess of the D'Urbervilles* (Torch Theatre), *The Taming of the Shrew* (Mappa Mundi), *Edward II* (FOD Theatre), *School for Scandal*, *Cloud Nine*, *Guys and Dolls*, *I Gofio Gwenlyn* and *Brand* (Bute Theatre). His television appearances include *Pubroom Paranoia*, *Middle English* and the BBC's *City Central*. Films include *Human Traffic* and *The Treatment*.

Neil Walls (Martin)

It started with singing – Neil loves to sing and was chosen at primary school to be one of the main characters in a show called *Factory Children* in which he sang solo. After this, Neil's school took part in an event for the new parliament house in Edinburgh which incorporated poems and songs presented by various schools. Neil's school was the only school to perform a play – *Maggie Robertson*. In between all this Neil had joined a group called Activate and the Whitehall Theatre Summer School. Neil's name has been on the waiting list to join the Rep's Junior Theatre Group – and here he is now!

Sharman Macdonald (Playwright)

Sharman's plays include *When I Was a Girl I Used to Scream and Shout* (produced at the Bush Theatre, Edinburgh International Festival and the West End, which won the Evening Standard Award for Most Promising Playwright), *The Brave* (produced at the Bush Theatre), *When We Were Women* (a National Theatre Studio commission produced at The Cottesloe and the Edinburgh International Festival), *All Things*

Nice (produced by the Royal Court, directed by Max Stafford-Clark), *Shades* (produced in the West End and directed by Simon Callow), *The Winter Guest* (a West Yorkshire Playhouse/Almeida Theatre co-production commissioned and directed by Alan Rickman), *Borders of Paradise* (Lou Stein's farewell production at Watford, nominated for the TMA Best Regional Play Award) and *Sea Urchins* (produced by Catherine Bailey Limited and directed by Richard Wilson for BBC Radio's 3 and 4, which won a Sony Award for Best Drama in 1997).

Her film work includes *Wild Flowers* (a Channel Four Film) and *The Winter Guest* (directed by Alan Rickman, starring Emma Thompson and Phyllida Law). Opera work includes *Hey Persephone!* (produced by Jonathan Reekie with music by Deirdre Gribbin for the Aldeburgh Festival and the Almeida Opera Season). Sharman has also written the novels *The Beast* and *Night Night* (published by Collins) and *Sharman Macdonald Plays One* (published by Faber and Faber and shortlisted for the McVities Scottish Writer of the Year Award).

Irina Brown (Director)

Irina grew up in Leningrad (St Petersburg). She started her career in Russia as a member of the avant-garde Theatre-Studio of Vladimir Malyshchitsky and ran her own company while at university. Since 1978 she has been living and working in Britain. She worked as Assistant Director to Andrei Tarkovsky, Yuri Lubimov and Anatoly Vassiliev. In 1985–87 she was a staff director at the

Royal National Theatre. Between 1983 and 1992 she also regularly worked as a staff producer at the Royal Opera House, Covent Garden. Irina joined the Tron Theatre as Artistic Director in 1996.

For the Tron Irina has directed *Lavochkin-5* by Alexei Shipenko (Mayfest 1997) and *Mate in Three* by Vittorio Franceschi. Other directing work includes *A Doll's House* (Birmingham Rep), the world premiere of *Blood Libel* by Arnold Wesker (Norwich Playhouse), *Romeo and Juliet* (Contact Theatre, Manchester), *A Midsummer Night's Dream* (Southern Shakespeare Festival, Florida), *The Sound of Music* (West Yorkshire Playhouse), *Our Country's Good* (Tabakov Theatre, Moscow), *The Misunderstanding* (Gate Theatre, Consummate Classics Season – winner of the Time Out/-01 for London Award 1990), *Peer Gynt* (Cambridge Arts Theatre, Marlowe Society Production), *Anton Chekhov* (Cottesloe, RNT, national tour and Jerusalem Festival).

Opera includes *Dido and Aeneas* (Royal Academy of Music) and directing revivals of Andrei Tarkovsky's production of *Boris Godunov* at the Royal Opera House and at the Kirov Opera, St Petersburg.

In 1993 she was Associate Director on the BAFTA Award-winning *Zinky Boys Go Underground*. She recently directed an English-language premiere of Ostrovsky's *More Sinned Against* in a version by Frank McGuinness for BBC Radio 3.

Jacqueline Gunn (Designer)

Jacqueline graduated from Wimbledon School of Art in 1982 and was awarded an Arts Council Bursary. As a result she became Assistant Designer at the Royal Opera House and with the Royal Shakespeare Company where she designed costumes for *The Dillen*. Jacqueline was the Associate Designer at Oldham Coliseum and then Resident Designer at Contact Theatre. Since becoming a freelance designer she has worked extensively throughout the UK and Europe.

In the world of dance she designed and co-devised a collaboration between Extemporary Dance and Westbrook Theatre. Other dance design includes *Virginia Minx at Play* with Emilyn Claid and the UK tour of *Akwaaba* for Adzido Pan-African Dance Ensemble.

Freelance theatre design includes *Krapp's Last Tape* (Bloomsbury Festival), *Twelfth Night* (Birmingham Rep), *The Tempest* (Kick Theatre), *A Pocket Dream* (Nottingham Playhouse and London West End), *Peer Gynt* (Cambridge, Marlowe Society), *Our Country's Good* (Tabakov Theatre, Moscow), *Blooding the Ocean* (Traverse Theatre), *Missing Mood Pants* (Regent's Park), *Cogs* (Circus Space).

Opera designs include *The Rake's Progress*, *La Voix Humaine* (both Bloomsbury Festival), *La Pietra del Paragone* (Wuppertal), *La Scala di Seta* and *L'Occasione Fa Il Ladro* (Wildbad Festival, Germany), *Tannhauser* (New Sussex Opera), *Labarinto* (Munich Biennale) and *Vaudeville* (Warsaw Music Festival), *Cosi Fan Tutte* (English National Opera). Jacqueline is currently designing *The Three Legged Table* (Slovenia).

Davy Cunningham
(Lighting Designer)

Davy was born in Scotland and studied philosophy at Stirling University. He has worked extensively in both theatre and opera and has lit over one hundred opera productions worldwide. Directors with whom he works frequently include Robert Carson, Dieter Kaegi and David Pountney.

West End includes Nicol Williamson's one man show *Jack* in 1994, Chekhov's *Ivanov* and Shakespeare's *Much Ado About Nothing* for Elijah Moshinsky at the Strand. Other theatre productions include *As You Like It* (Nottingham Playhouse), *Charlie's Aunt* (Royal Exchange), *The Maiden Stone, Hansel and Gretel* (Royal Lyceum Theatre Company) and *Julius Caesar* (Birmingham Repertory Theatre). Future theatre productions are *Angel Magick* (Salisbury Playhouse), the BBC Proms, *Snow Queen* (Royal Lyceum).

Opera productions include seven productions at the English National Opera including *The Excursions of Mr Brouchek* (also Bavarian State Opera), *A Midsummer Night's Dream* (also Aix-en-Provence, Ravenna Festival, Turin and Strasbourg) and *The Mikado* (also Houston, Texas); thirteen works for Opera North including *Julietta* in 1997 (also Opera Zuid 1998); six productions for Scottish Opera including *Norma* in 1997; *Cendrillon* (Welsh National Opera, also Monte Carlo, Turin, Toulouse and Antwerp). Future plans include *Dalibor* (Scottish Opera, Edinburgh Festival), *La Bohème* (Göteborg), *Pique Dame* (Antwerp).

John Irvine (Musical Director)

John Irvine is an Edinburgh based composer who is completing a PhD in Music Composition at Edinburgh University. His theatre work includes *White Bird Passes* (Dundee Rep Theatre), *Lavochkin–5* (Tron Theatre), *Moscow Stations, Unidentified Human Remains, Poor Super Man* (Traverse, Hampstead and Union Square Theatre New York), *Widows, Reader, Europe, The Struggle of the Dogs and the Black, Columbus, The Life of Stuff, Buchanan, Brothers of Thunder, The Hope Slide* (Traverse), *Trainspotting* (Citizen's, Bush and Traverse), *Quiet Night In* (KtC), *The New Menoza* (Gate) and *Seven-Tenths* (Walk the Plank).

Ros Steen (Dialect Coach)

Ros trained at RSAMD. Theatre work includes *The Chic, Lazybed, Knives in Hens, Passing Places, Bondagers, Road to Nirvana, Sharp Shorts, Marisol, Grace in America, Brothers of Thunder* (Traverse Theatre), *The Dying Gaul, Conversation with a Cupboard Man, Eva Peron, Long Day's Journey into Night, Shadow of a Gunman, A Taste of Honey, The Tinker's Wedding, Riders to the Sea* (Citizens'), *Odysseus Thump* (West Yorkshire Playhouse), *Babycakes* (Clyde Unity), *Abigail's Party* (Perth Rep), *Pygmalion, Our Country's Good, Armstrong's Last Stand* (Royal Lyceum), *Trainspotting* (G and J Productions), *The Hanging Tree, Laundry, Entertaining Angels* (LookOut), *Sunset Song* (TAG), *Bold Girls* (Theatre Galore). Film work includes *Stella Does Tricks*. Television work includes *Hamish Macbeth, Looking after Jo Jo, St Anthony's Day Off, Changing Step*.

The Tron Theatre and Company

The Tron Theatre Company was established in 1985 when
Michael Boyd was appointed as the first Artistic Director of the
Tron Theatre. In 1996 Michael Boyd left the Tron to join the
Royal Shakespeare Company as an Associate Director. In
December 1996, Irina Brown joined the Tron as Artistic Director.
Sea Urchins is her third production with the Tron Theatre
Company and her first co-production with Dundee Rep.

Highlights of the Company's work include: *Mate in Three* by
Vittorio Franceschi; the UK premiere of Alexei Shipenko's
Lavochkin-5; three productions by Quebecois writer Michel
Tremblay: *The Guid Sisters, Hosanna* and *The Real Wurld?*; the
adaptation of Janice Galloway's *The Trick is to Keep Breathing*;
C.P. Taylor's *Good* and *Macbeth* by William Shakespeare. The
Company has also featured the work of writers Peter Arnott,
Chris Hannan, David Kane, Forbes Masson and Tony Roper.

The Tron Theatre Company has toured to Canada to take part
in Les Celebrations du Montreal 350 and twice performed at
Toronto's prestigious Du Maurier International Festival, as well
as being invited to the Stoneybrook Arts Festival in New York,
U.S.A. The Company has won six Mayfest Scotland on Sunday
Paper Boat Awards, including Best Actor for Miriam Karlin's
performance in *Lavochkin-5*. *Dumbstruck* won the Writers Guild
Award for Best New Play and the LWT Plays on Stage Award.

In addition to the work of the Tron Theatre Company, the Tron
Theatre also presents the best of touring theatre, comedy and
music from Scotland, the UK and abroad.

Tron Staff

Production

Irina Brown	Artistic Director
Lorenzo Mele	Associate Director, Bruce Millar Award
Susan Worsfold	RSAMD Trainee Director
Jo Masson	Production Manager
Malcolm Rogan	Technical Manager
Shaun Luckly	Deputy Technical Manager

Administration

Neil Murray	Administrative Director
Kate Bell	Bookkeeper
Pat Miller	Bookkeeper
Gwen Stewart	Administration Assistant

Redevelopment of the Tron Theatre

The Tron Theatre occupies a unique place in Glasgow's cultural and architectural heritage. The current capital development led by architects RMJM Scotland will create an exciting architectural ensemble of new buildings while at the same time preserving and enhancing the beautiful 'A' Listed historic structure. The first completed phase of the building can now be seen and visited. The new box office, wrapped inside J. J. Burnet's 1899 screen wall, offers an excellent perspective of the eighteenth-century John Adam Church at the heart of the theatre as well as a view of the original sixteenth-century Tron steeple, Glasgow's third oldest structure.

The second phase of work will provide a new bar and kitchens as well as administration and production offices and will be completed by the end of summer 1998. This will further enhance the Tron's reputation as one of Glasgow's great eating and drinking venues, as well as the city's most eclectic theatre.

The final phase of work will provide the Tron with a much needed rehearsal/workshop studio, as well as making major improvements to the auditorium. This work will take place between August 1998 and March 1999, and will mean that there will be no events in the auditorium during this period. However, we intend to keep the profile of the Tron alive by programming exciting events in unusual spaces within the building until the development is completed.

Sea Urchins is therefore the last chance to see the Tron in its current shape. We hope you keep coming to see us while the work continues and look forward to welcoming you to the new, improved Tron.

The Tron redevelopment is funded by the Scottish Arts Council National Lottery Fund, Strathclyde European Partnership, and Glasgow City Council.

Glasgow

Dundee
City Council
Arts and Heritage

STRATHCLYDE
european
PARTNERSHIP

THE SCOTTISH ARTS COUNCIL

NATIONAL LOTTERY FUND

Dundee Rep Theatre

Dundee Rep has been established since 1939 and has been housed in its award-winning purpose built premises since 1983.

The Rep is a unique organisation in the UK, providing the most comprehensive arts service in Scotland. Made up of three major elements, it embraces not only an acclaimed theatre programme, but is home to Scottish Dance Theatre – Scotland's largest full-time contemporary dance company – and a hugely successful Community Department which incorporates three further elements. The Community Drama Department has a significant relationship with the local community, and both the Specialist Dramatherapy Service (the only such service within the UK that is attached to a theatre) and the Arts Advocacy Project, provide innovative therapy programmes for people with mental health problems.

As a producing house, Dundee Rep Theatre stages its own productions and offers a repertoire of great drama from throughout the world. It commissions the best playwrights to write new work and to translate and adapt classical texts to be relevant to the contemporary, cultural or social climate in Scotland today. Over recent years the Rep has gone from strength to strength, developing its audience and gaining both public and critical acclaim. In 1996 it went on to receive the TMA Martini Award for the Best Overall Production in the UK for *On the Line – a Celebration of Timex in Dundee* by Alan Spence.

It also acts as a presenting house, hosting work from the best visiting companies from throughout Scotland and the UK, thereby providing audiences with an eclectic mix of high quality drama, folk, jazz and pop music, classical and contemporary dance, children's theatre, opera and musicals.

Dundee Rep Staff

Sinclair Aitken . . . . Chairman of the Board of Directors
Hamish Glen . . . . Artistic Director
Joanna Reid . . . . Administrative Director

Administration

Helen Watson . . . . Administration Manager
Helen Smith . . . . Theatre Accountant
Eileen Langlands . . . . Accounts Assistant
Tina Herd . . . . Office Junior

Front of House

Denise Winford . . . . Marketing Manager
Nicola Young . . . . Press & Publicity Officer

Nicola Gibson . . . . Front of House Manager
Lena Howie, Barclay Dakers, Chris Wright . . . . Front of House Relief
Joyce Sowden . . . . Box Office Manager
Sharon Morwood, David Young . . . . Box Office Assistants
Lena Howie . . . . Front of House Supervisor
Nick Wright . . . . Het Theatercafé Manager
Stephen Murray . . . . Head Chef
Stewart Norrie . . . . Cleaning Supervisor

Production

John Miller . . . . Production Manager
Anna Newall . . . . SAC Associate Director
Richard Baron . . . . Associate Artist
Dave Nicol . . . . Technical Manager
Linda Kyle . . . . Stage Manager
Niki Ewen . . . . Deputy Stage Manager
Hilly, Viktoria Begg . . . . Assistant Stage Managers
Alison Muir, Angie McGregor . . . . Chaperones
John Farmer . . . . Stage Technician
Neil Goodwill . . . . Chief Electrician
Andrew Meadows . . . . Deputy Electrician
Pat Burns . . . . Assistant Carpenter
Andrew Morrison . . . . Design Assistant/Scenic Artist
Pauline Ord . . . . Assistant Scenic Artist
Phyllis Byrne . . . . Wardrobe Supervisor
Lyndie Macintyre . . . . Deputy Wardrobe Supervisor
Irene Phillip . . . . Wardrobe Maintenance

Scottish Dance Theatre

Janet Smith . . . . Artistic Director
Amanda Chinn . . . . Senior Administrator
Amanda Roberts . . . . Administrator
Errol White . . . . Rehearsal Director/Dancer
Alan David Brooks, Davina Givan,
Michael Lindo, Rachel Morrow . . . . Dancers
Stephen Prickett . . . . Dance Worker
Steve Mackie . . . . Technical Stage Manager
Craig Harrower . . . . Stage Technician

Community Department

Michael Duke . . . . Associate Director
Joyce Milne . . . . Community Administrator
Mark Oakley . . . . Drama Worker
Genevieve Smyth . . . . Dramatherapist
Paul McQuade . . . . Dramatherapy Admin Assistant
Aileen Taylor . . . . Arts Advocacy Administrator

Corporate Patrons

Bank of Scotland   Royal & Sun Alliance, UK Commercial
James Keiller Estates Ltd   Willis Corroon

Past Sponsors

Bank of Scotland   Telewest Communications
Cox Johnson   Tetley Alloa
Selan Design

Sharman Macdonald
Sea Urchins

ff

faber and faber

LONDON · BOSTON

First published in 1998
by Faber and Faber Limited
3 Queen Square London WC1N 3AU

Typeset by Country Setting, Woodchurch, Kent TN26 3TB
Printed in England by Intype London Ltd

A CIP record for this book
is available from the British Library

ISBN 0–571–19695–0

2 4 6 8 10 9 7 5 3 1

Characters

Martin An English boy. Twelve or thereabouts

Rena A Scottish girl. Eleven

Ailsa Her mother

John Ailsa's Welsh husband

David John's brother

Dora David's wife

Gareth Their son. Twenty-one

Rhiannon Gareth's sister. Eighteen

Noelle Rhiannon's sister. Rena's cousin. Eleven

Man A Glaswegian

The play itself exists because of Catherine Bailey.
She asked me to write a radio play for
Catherine Bailey Ltd – whatever I wanted.
I hadn't ever thought of writing one.
If she hadn't asked *Sea Urchins* wouldn't exist.
Irina Brown heard it and decided to put it on stage.

The play is set on a coved, pebbled beach,
below a cliff near David's home
on the Atlantic Coast of Wales.

The music is as I remember it.
There must be sheet music somewhere
that would mend the idiosyncrasies of memory.

Any incidental music should be Hawaiian guitar.

The slashes and asterisks are borrowed
from Caryl Churchill: / indicates an interruption;
* indicates that the dialogue travels from star to star.

Act One

Distant shushing of the waves on pebbles.

Feet rushing. Pebbles rolling. Martin slipping and slithering over the slopes of the beach, looking for his brother. Yelling. His yells make the place vast and empty.

Rena's watching.

Martin   George! George. George!

Twists an ankle.

Damn. Damn. Damn. Damn.

Runs on.

George.

When he's gone Rena twists round onto her back. Looks up into the vast blue of the sky. She's lying in a pebble hollow. Rough sea grass blows around her. A private voice.

Rena   Aberrhyll. That's where I am.

In the distance Martin's running feet.

OK Mr Manning? June 16th. 1961. Synchronise watches. Three, two, one. Eight a.m. precisely. There are white horses on the waves and the weather's fine. Mr Manning? I'm calling you. They say you're the best. A clean killer. Is that not right? A man of business. I read the papers. Even the police, my Dad says. They speak of you with awe in their voices. You've got to leave Glasgow right away and get yourself down here. Aberrhyll. The beach below the cliff. Have you got that?

I'm at the end of my tether. You're my last hope. Mr Manning, I've got some business for you.

Martin's feet clatter across the stones. Closer and closer. He doesn't see Rena. She doesn't see him. Flesh bumps on flesh. Rena yells.

Mind it.

Martin   Sorry.

Rena   That's just a word.

Martin stares. Rena stares back. It's a stand off.

Rena   Well?

Martin   What?

Rena   See me, see Beethoven.

Martin   What?

Rena   Don't you understand English?

Martin   Beethoven?

Rena   It's rude to stare. Did your mother never tell you that? I haven't got time for this. Go away. Go on, get.

She watches him back off up the beach. Goes back to her private voice.

Please forgive the interruption, Mr Manning. Some boy that's all. I don't know him. He's not part of it.

Martin's staring from a safe distance.

I don't want any mistakes. See me before you murder anyone. I'm the boss. I'm still feeling a bit sick but fully compus mentus, so don't you go trying anything off your own bat. I spewed up three times on the drive down but I managed to get out of the car. So no one was cross with me. We'll have a Hillman next year by the way if we're all still alive. There are hermits on the Rest and Be Thankful. Which I was glad to see. That's where I'm headed if you fail. I'd rather be a hermit than on this beach waiting for Noelle to get here. She's it Mr Manning. Kill her. She's the same age as me, only she's got breasts but. Note that down in indelible pencil Mr Manning. B.R.E.A.S.T.S. God help me I never hear the end of them. Of course we may be talking about a multiple killing Mr Manning. We'll see how the day pans out. Families Mr Manning. They're the very devil at the best of times. But on holiday they really do take the biscuit. Payment will be by IOU. I intend to be rich in my own right by the time I'm twenty-five. So you can collect then, provided you've not been hanged / OK Mr Manning? OK? OK?

Ailsa's walking down the beach. She calls to Martin.

Ailsa Hello there.

Martin Hello.

His reply catches Rena's attention. He ducks down into a hollow. Creeps round nearer to her.

Ailsa laughs in delight at the wind in her hair and the warmth and the blue blue day.

Rena's watching Ailsa from her hollow.

Rena That's my mum Mister Manning. She's part of it. Not the worst part. Not by a long chalk.

Ailsa's right at the sea's edge. The gentle waves push at the stones at her feet.

Ailsa Oh yes. / Yes, yes.

Rena's watching Ailsa.

Rena (*whispers*) Oh God. Oh no. Oh shite.

7

Ailsa begins to sing. Her voice embraces the whole coastline.

Ailsa

There'll be a / welcome in the hillside.

Rena   (*whispers*) Christ, don't sing.

Ailsa calls.

Ailsa   Come down here John.

John's in the grassy wind-sheltered cove far behind her. He's filling the primus with paraffin. The fuel glugs into the base of the stove. Metal grinds against metal.

John   God save us.

He pumps up the fuel with the metal plunger.

Ailsa   (*calls*) Come on and I'll hold your hand by the sea's edge and we'll pretend we're winchin'.

John   (*calls*) I'm doing something en' I. Sing your song Ailsa. (*to himself*) Let's get it over with.

Ailsa's voice is high, strong and Scottish. She's gloriously sentimental.

Ailsa

There'll be a welcome in the dale
This land of ours will / still be singing*

The song continues.

Rena   (*whispers*) Shut up. Shut up. Jesus.

Rena wriggles forward on her stomach. A bird cries.

Ailsa

* When you come home / again to Wales.

Rena   (*whispers*) Shut up, shut up, shut up, shut up.

Martin's foot slithers on the shingle. An intake of breath. A loose stone slithers and clatters down the slope.

Martin Hey!

The stone hits Rena on the shoulder.

Rena Jesus. Did you throw that?

Martin slithers down the stony slope.

Martin It was an accident.

Rena Clumsy wee shite.

Martin I shouted.

Rena I had my fingers in my ears.

Martin It was only a pebble.

Rena It was a rock by the way.

Rena twists round to look at her shoulder.

I've got a bruise.

Martin Can I see?

Rena Help yourself.

Martin crunches across the stones.

Martin It's quite big.

Rena You don't have to prod it do you?

Martin Looks sore.

Rena I bruise easily.

Martin That'll be your hair.

Rena What's wrong with it?

Martin People with red hair bruise easily.

Rena D'you want a punch in the mouth?

Martin Delicate skin that's all. Red hair.

Rena Auburn.

Martin I don't dislike it.

Rena That's big of you.

Ailsa's singing reaches them from the sea's edge.

Ailsa
They'll take away each hour of heiryth
When you come home again to Wales.

Martin She looks sad.

Rena Mind your own business.

Martin She's very attractive.

Rena Eh?

Martin Like mother, like daughter.

Rena D'you mean that for a compliment?

Martin She is your mother isn't she?

Rena Oh my God.

Martin What?

Rena She's stopped. Silence. Feel the smell of it.

Martin You can't smell silence.

Rena I can. Don't you just love it.

A bird cries. The wind blows. The waves break on the beach.

Martin The waves make quite a racket.

Rena See that song. She sings that for my father. I'm never going to be a woman.

Martin   D'you come here every year?

Rena   Every year of my whole life.

George begins to cry. Martin's head turns.

Rena   Who's that?

Martin   George.

Rena   Who?

Martin   My brother.

Rena   That's sore crying.

Martin   He starts sometimes and he can't stop.

Rena   We all have our burdens in this world. You have yours and I have mine.

John calls down from the cove.

John   Rena!

Martin   That your / dad?

Rena   Your brother's breaking his / heart.

Martin   Aren't you / going?

Rena   See him. See him crying. Takes the soul out of you, that. Can't you stop him?

Martin   My mother can.

The crying turns to sobbing.

See.

The sobs lessen.

Rena   He must love her.

Martin   Would you like to come swimming with me?

Rena studies him quite carefully. Till he can't meet her look.

I mean, if you want.

She's about to answer, on the edge of a smile.

John   (*calls*) Get yourself over here.

Rena runs off. Her feet sliding on the stones.

Rena   Aw. Jesus, Jesus, Jesus.

John   (*calls*) Shift, Rena.

Martin yells after her.

Martin   What's your name?

Rena   You stupid or what are you?

John   (*calls*) Rena!

Rena   The whole of bloody Wales knows my name.

Martin   Rena?

Rena   What, for God's sake?

Martin   See you later?

Rena   Alright.

Martin   Promise?

Rena   Uh huh.

Martin runs over the stones.

See him, Mr Manning? Don't you lay a finger on him.
Do you hear me?

John   (*calls*) Chop chop. Banana banana.

*In the cove John plays the introduction to Leadbelly's
'Good Morning Blues'. Rena runs over the stones
onto the grass. Throws herself down.*

John   You took your time.

Fat spits in the frying pan. The primus roars. There's an angry sizzle as bacon hits the fat. Martin's creeping round so that he can watch them.

Ailsa Why can't they get here first? Why can't they do that?*

John sings.

John
Good morning Blues
Blues how / do you do?
Good morning blues
Blues how do you do?

Ailsa * They'll get here when the bacon's right crisp and not a moment before. Then they'll thunder up, the whole damn herd of them. Why should this year be any different?

Rena You like them though.*

John
I'm doing alright
Good morning how are you?

The guitar plays on.

Ailsa * There's no surprise in my life and very little pleasure.

Rena Don't say that.

Ailsa When I was wee we went to Dunbar for the Glasgow Fair fortnight and your grandfather hired a cottage and we took your grandmother's charlady with us. Auntie Mac. She cooked the breakfast. Look at me. I've come down in the world.*

John You've come down in the world?

Ailsa * Never marry a Welshman.

John I sold my birthright for a plate of porridge.

Ailsa My father ate his porridge with salt and put pepper on his strawberries. He suffered from kidney stones. From the rhubarb they said. Your grandmother's rhubarb was legendary. There's nothing legendary about your father's family. They're Methodists.

Rena Say you like coming here.

Ailsa I come here for him.

Rena Say it. Please.

Ailsa Oh my God.

Rena What is it? What's wrong?

Ailsa Bloody bacon spat in my eye. / God's greatest invention was the electric cooker. And I'm down on my hunkers at a bloody primus stove arguing with a rasher of streaky.*

John
  I laid down last night
  Turning from side to side
  I laid down last night
  Turning from side to side.

  Speaks.

Pick up your guitar Rena. Rena I need you.

  Fingers slide on the strings.

Ailsa * I'll have a bloodspot. Is that inflamed is it?

John C. C. That's D. C.*

  Another guitar strums almost in rhythm.

Ailsa I could be dying here for God's Sake.

John sings.

John
* But I wasn't sick.
Just / dissatisfied.

Ailsa John?

John I woke up this morning
Blues sneaking round my head
I woke up this morning.

Speaks.

C. D. G.

Sings.

Blues sneaking round my head.

Speaks.

G. G, Rena. G.

Sings.

I couldn't eat
Blues all in my bread.

Speaks.

That's not a left hand Rena. That's a rollmop herring.

John picks. Rena strums.

Ailsa You drive that girl too hard.

John She's my harp of joy.

Ailsa Is that what she is?

John Don't you listen to / your mother Rena.*

Ailsa Have I smudged my mascara? Have I?

John sings.

John
    * She's driving me crazy /
    What am I going to do?

Ailsa   He thinks* he's awful funny.

Rena   Your mascara's fine.

John
    * She's driving me crazy
    What am I going to do?
    I ain't got nobody
    To take my troubles to.

C, Rena. C, Rena. C. C. C. You glean knowledge in this world.

Ailsa   Here we go.

John   It may not be much but it's all I have to leave you Rena. The knowledge that I've gleaned.

Ailsa   Planning on dying are you?

John   Who knows what the future holds?

Ailsa   We've a long way to go yet, you and me.

John   Not so long as we've been.

Ailsa   Planning on leaving me?

John
    You're driving me crazy
    What am I going to do?

Ailsa   I'm asking you a question John Williams.

    John sings.

John
    I need somebody
    To take my troubles to.

His voice fades. His picking fades. Rena's stuttering strum comes to the fore and her private voice.

Rena Manning come here and murder me where I sit. I'd like that. Manning. Mr Manning. They're at their damn games again. Don't leave me to listen to them. Come on now. Right now.

She whisper-sings. Still in the private voice.

Come on Mr Manning
You can murder me any time
Come on Mr Manning
You can murder me any time
Cause I'll be so glad
To be your number nine.

Strings jar.

John What do you call that?

Rena What?

John Don't look at your fingers. What's that chord? Know it in your soul Rena.

Rena G? G seventh. It's D seventh. D seventh, Dad. Sorry. Sorry.

John What should it be?

Rena C?

John Don't ask me. Tell me.

Rena I don't know. / I don't know.

Ailsa She can't play.

John You've never strummed anything more than a bloody ukelele, Ailsa. / Don't you start talking to me about the guitar.

Ailsa You can't put there what's not there in the first place. / Practise she ever so.

John I thank God for one thing.

Ailsa What's that John Williams?

John She hasn't inherited your voice.* On my bended knees I thank God for that.

Rena's private voice whispers through the bitter words.

Rena Manning come on. Come on quick. I need you Manning. I need you now.

Ailsa * I'm warning you John. / We both know you can hurt me.

John I'll tell you something about your voice. It's not this world it belongs to. And I'm not talking about angels. Your voice belongs in the other place Ailsa. Buried deep.

Ailsa You always preferred a contralto. / You've made that perfectly obvious.

Rena Don't. Don't, don't / don't don't.

Ailsa He likes your Auntie Doe's voice best. Amongst all the other things he likes about your Auntie Doe. / And I'm not talking about her Welsh cakes.

John Enough.

Ailsa It's the God's honest truth.

John Truth tellers are the salt of the earth and they should be buried in it for the harm that they do.*

Rena's whispering.

Rena God Manning. Stop them. Stop them.

Ailsa * You're a romantic John Williams.

John   Romantic / am I?

Ailsa   Whatever you can't have. That's what your heart desires.

John   You tell me something Ailsa. If I'm romantic how come I married you?

Ailsa   That's cheap.

John   You should know.

Ailsa   A true singer sings with her heart. And when the heart goes out of her she sings no more. I'm begging you to leave me with something John.

John   This is not about you.

Ailsa   I'm what you've got. Nobody twisted your damn arm. I'm what you've got. You tell me. Out loud. So that it's in the air between us. I'm what you've got. What is it that you cling to? Answer me that. As if I didn't know. My God, I wish I didn't know.

John   Pick up the guitar Rena.

Ailsa   Leave her.

John   Pick it up Rena.

Rena   My fingers are sore.

John   Feel. Feel there. Tips of my fingers. Callouses, see. Feel how hard they are. Your fingers will be like that one day. They won't hurt you then.

Rena   I'm no good at the guitar.

John   You will be.

Ailsa   How will she?

John   One day. When I'm gone and you've got a man of your own Rena. That you'll love and care for more than you ever have me. You'll play for him. And your children Rena. You'll teach them what I've taught you. See this. Feel it. Feel the sun on the wood. That's my Gibson Kalamazoo you're touching there.

Rena   I won't marry.

John   You will.

Rena   I won't leave you.

Ailsa   I used to say that to my Father.* I'd sit on his knee, I'd clap his head. He'd give me anything I wanted. The moon from out of the sky he'd give me on a plate or a new silk dance dress from Pettigrew and Stevens.

John   * You'll leave me and my name will go out of this world.

Rena   There's Gareth, isn't there?

John   He bears your Uncle David's name.

Rena   Same difference.

John   Not to me. See my guitar. This is what you'll have, Rena Maeve. All through your life you'll have it. And when I die I'll die happy knowing that you've got my guitar and the skill to play it. That's what'll be left of me on this earth when I leave it. Ring finger, E string, third fret.

A steel string complains.

Ailsa   Rena Maeve'll be left will she? Rena Maeve and your Gibson Kalamazoo?

John   Enough, Ailsa.

Ailsa   Is that all that'll be left?

John   I'm warning you.

Ailsa   You're not the clean potato John Williams.

The hissing and sparking of the bacon fades. Rena whisper-sings.

Rena
Dear Mr Manning
Hear me calling to you
Dear Mr Manning
Hear me calling to you
I've got some troubles
You can help me through.*

The guitar stumbles.

John Don't fight it darling. It's your lover, not your killer.

The guitar hits a smooth patch.

You're my daughter and you're special. Never you forget that. You can do anything you want in this life. Be anything that you want. You just have to want, Rena Maeve. You just have to want.

Rena
* Pick up your knife now
Plunge it in to my breast
Pick up your knife now
Plunge it in to my breast
I got the blues Mr Manning
I need to get me some rest.

Rena's guitar stutters on. John's joins.

David, Dora, Gareth, Rhiannon and Noelle Williams walk along the cliff path. The wind's blowing up there. The grass is rustling. The music's distant.

David He's got her playing.

Gareth What's she playing on?

David He'll have made her that.

Gareth You can't tell that from up here.

David Left handed guitar Gareth. Done no less for her than I did for you.

Gareth She can't play Da.

David Sausages for fingers.

Noelle Oh God these summers. These summers.

Dora Don't be affected Noelle Williams. I never liked an affected child.

Noelle You telling me you're looking forward to it are you Mam?

David It's family right. Right Noelle? Right?

Noelle Ttttt.

David You'll behave Noelle. I'm not asking you, I'm telling you.

Noelle I'm promising nothing.

Gareth You let her away with murder.

David Nothing wrong with a bit of spirit.

Dora When they were babies that was the best time. I only ever wanted babies. Catch up Rhiannon. Come on.

Noelle I'll get her.

Noelle runs down the sunbaked mud cliff path.
Dora calls.

Dora Not so fast Noelle.

Noelle runs at Rhiannon.

Noelle Rhia aa aa non.

Rhiannon For God's sake.

Noelle charges into Rhiannon. Knocks the breath out of her.

Stupid cow.

Noelle's laughing.

Noelle Joke Rhiannon.

Rhiannon You could've bloody killed me.

Noelle How could I?

Rhiannon You're no light weight Noelle. Suppose I'd gone over?

Noelle You'd be lying squashed at the bottom of the cliff and there'd be one less nuisance in the world. You think you're so great.

Pause.

You're up to something Rhiannon Williams.

Rhiannon Don't talk daft.

Noelle You want watching.

Rhiannon You've got an over-active imagination.

Noelle Sweetness and light they think you are. I know better. You're waiting for someone.

Rhiannon I am not.

Noelle What're you looking up there for?

Rhiannon Cliff's beautiful in the sunlight.

Noelle Since when have you been a nature lover, Rhia Williams?

Dora calls.

Dora Come on you two. Don't lag. Gareth, go and make them come can't you?

David   You're alright aren't you Dora?

Dora   'Course I am. Why shouldn't I be?

David   You'd tell me wouldn't you?

Dora   Tell you what Dai?

David   I don't know.

Dora   Well if you don't know, heart, how should I?

David   If you weren't alright you'd tell me. If you were sad like?

Dora   * What have I got to be sad about? On a day like today? I've got nothing on this earth to be sad about Dai. Neither have you, my love. Neither have you.

And she walks on down the hill into the music in the cove.

John
    * Blues you're driving me crazy
    What am I going to do?
    I ain't got nobody
    To take my troubles to.

Rena!

A sequence of chord changes more or less in rhythm, rather less stumbling than they have been. John puts a two chord stop on it. Applause.

Dora   Clever, / clever girl.

Rena   Don't Auntie Doe.

David   True member of this family / you've got here John.*

John   Four guitars we / can muster now.

Rena   * I can't play.

David No such word.

Rena I'm useless Uncle David. You know that better than anyone.

She runs. John calls after her.

John Rena?

Gareth Women!

Martin slides out from his hiding place in the grass and follows Rena. The bacon sizzles.

Ailsa You can have bacon. You can have black pudding. You can have sausages. / Gareth, look at the height of you.

Dora Spoiling us Ailsa heart.

Ailsa You look well Doe.

Rhiannon Good to see you Auntie Ailsa.

Ailsa She's growing into the family look. I see my husband in your eyes Rhiannon. She's John's eyes Doe. God help us all. You see your age in the young ones Dora.

Dora See your age in the faces of your friends Ailsa. Least that's where I see mine.

Ailsa I hope that's not me you're referring to.

Gareth The whole world fancies you Auntie Ailsa, specially when there's bacon on the primus.

Ailsa You're a sweet talker.

Dora I could live in Scotland for their baps. Though the people scare me to death.

Ailsa Of course Wales is famous for it's saints, Dora.

Dora Is that a fact?

Ailsa   You should know.

Dora   I beg your pardon.

Ailsa   You've your own Welsh saint that you're married to.

Dora   I'll have my bacon well done.

Ailsa   It's always good to see you in the flesh Dora.

Dora   I look forward to your visits.

Ailsa   There's a masochist in all of us then.

David   Girls. Girls.

Ailsa   Is that well enough done for you?

Dora   You were always a good cook.

Ailsa   I have many talents Dora. Many, many, many.

Dora   We must all thank God for that.

Ailsa   Your wife doesn't change David.

Gareth   You give as good as you get Auntie Ailsa. You always have.

The sizzle of bacon fades into the sound of the sea and the cry of a bird.

Rena runs along the beach. Lies down flat on the stones. She's crying.

Martin stops running when he sees her. Listens to her crying. Walks softly over to her. Stands looking down at her. Rena stifles her sobs.

Martin   You crying?

Rena   Feel the stones. You could fry eggs on them. Don't you just love the heat. I haven't a hankie.

Martin   Here.

Rena   Jesus. The bloody thing's clean. Mammy's boy. Won't even say shite. I hate Mammy's boys. You can't trust them.

Martin   Shite.

She applauds.

Rena   There's a big man.

Martin   I'm not the one crying.

Rena   I get bad hay fever sometimes.

An English woman's voice calls.

Maureen   Martin?

Rena   That you is it? Martin? That your Mother calling you?

Martin   She just wants to know where I am.

Rena   Wave then. There's a sweetheart.

She starts to laugh.

Martin   What's funny?

Rena   Martin?

Martin   So what?

Rena   She can't have liked you much, your mother, to have called you that.

Martin   Are you always like this?

Rena   Say I wasn't crying.

Martin   'I wasn't crying.'

Rena   You weren't crying say.

Pause.

27

Bugger you then . . . Martin. You're an awful Nosey Parker by the way. You were watching us weren't you. You were in the grass spying on us. Don't think I didn't see you. What's the big fascination, eh?

Martin   We don't play guitars in my family.

Rena   What do you do?

Martin   We play board games on Sunday afternoons.

Rena   Monopoly?

Martin   Ludo.

Rena   I quite like Ludo.

Martin   I like guitars.

Pause.

Rena   Why does she hold your brother like that, your mum?

Martin   Don't you like being held?

Rena   Depends who's doing the holding.

Beat.

What's wrong with your brother Martin?

Martin   My mum and dad were too old to have another child. That's what the girls down my road say. They say it's disgusting at their age and they got what they deserved.

Rena   Girls can be cruel.

Martin   George is alright.

Rena   I'm cruel.

Martin   I know.

Rena   Why do you like me then?

Martin   What were you crying for?

Rena   My cousin's imminent. Noelle, for she was born on Christmas day. So she started out special. Doesn't that make you sick. If you like me. You mustn't like her. Promise.

   Pause.

Martin   Where is she?

Rena   She takes her own sweet time about everything. She's spoilt. People think only children are spoilt. They're not. See only children, they have an onerous burden on their shoulders. They're never spoilt. I can always tell an only child.

Martin   Is that what you are?

Rena   See skeletons. They're supposed to stay in cupboards by the way. See our skeletons, they keep popping out to join the party.* They're particularly fond of Wales.

   Up in the grassy cove one guitar's strumming. John's singing.

John
   Out in Arizona where the bad men are
   And the only friend to guide you is an evening star
   The roughest, toughest man by far
   Is ragtime cowboy Joe.
   He got his name by singing to the cows and sheep
   Every night they say he sings his herd to sleep
   In a voice so rich and deep
   Creening soft and low
   * He used to sing
   Raggy music to the cattle as he swings
   Back and forward in a saddle on a horse
   That is syncopated gaited

29

And there's such a funny meter
To the roar of his repeater
How they run
When they hear that feller's gun
Because the western folk all know

Three guitars picking and strumming.

He's a hi falutin' rootin' tootin'
Son of a gun from Arizona
Rag time cowboy
Dirty old cowboy
Rag time cowboy Joe.

They go from 'Cowboy Joe' into 'The Hawaiian War Chant'. Gareth's singing. The men are the chorus. The steel string modulates to a bottle-neck Hawaiian sound.

Gareth
Hic a hooera
A tac a hac a hooera
Hic a hooera
A tac a hac a hooera
O wooera

David and **John**
Wuh, wuh, wuh

Gareth
Hic a hooera

David and **John**
Wuh, wuh, wuh

Gareth
O wooera

David and **John**
Wuh, wuh, wuh

Gareth
Hic a hooera

David and **John**
Wuh, wuh, wuh.

David Doe-Doe. With me now.

Romantic slow slides on the guitar.

Dora
Sing me a song of the islands
My serenade where the trade winds blow
Sing me a song of the islands*
Where hearts are high and the moon is low.

Ailsa calls down from the cove to the beach.

Ailsa * Rena, I've a roll for you.

Rhiannon joins Dora in harmony.

Both
Where rippling waters seem to sa aaaa yeee*
Oh ah oh ee alleee ayeee.
Bring me the / fragrance of ginger
Strum your guitars while I sing away
Sing me a song of the islands
Oh ah oh ee allleee ayee.

A wave breaks. The guitars are in the distance and the singing. The stones crunch under Rena's feet.

Martin * Don't go.

Rena I'll be back.

He calls after her.

Martin What's their burden, only children?

Rena Their parents, for God's sake.

Martin My mother said George'll be the saving of me.

31

Rena   Do you need saving?

Martin   From her she said. I've always to protect him and stand up for him. The neighbours say his death would be a mercy. 'After all,' they say. 'He's quite sweet now,' they say. 'He won't be so sweet at six-foot-four and still in nappies.' The men in our family achieve a great height.

Rena   The men in our family play the guitar. The women sing. I'm genetically unsound so they tell me for I do neither.

Martin   I heard you playing.

Rena   I can't play. I'm a disappointment. Noelle's never disappointed in her life.

Martin   You sounded alright to me.

Rena   It's just a noise, music. Leadbelly and Brownie Mcghee, they're a noise. My Dad plays me Beethoven on the gramophone. Tchaikovsky he plays. Bach. It's a noise and it hurts my ears. See. In any other family it wouldn't matter. I'm a changeling in their nest. My hair's a flag that signifies that. I'm left-handed for God's sake. The devil took their proper child. My mother didn't see me for two days after I was born. My birth was very tiring. Noelle says I was swapped.

Martin   She's teasing you.

Rena   She's torturing me. That's her speciality.

Martin   Don't listen to her.

Rena   Everyone listens to Noelle. Even the skeletons dance to her tune.

Waves pull the stones down the slope to the sea.

In the cove.

John Heart's ease. Rhiannon my love. Give your old uncle a treat.

Rhiannon You're not old.

John Do you still cry when you sing?

Rhiannon That's my curse.

John Come on my child.

Rhiannon I'm no child.

John You are to me.

Four soft chords.

Rhiannon
Lu la lu la lu la lu la
Bye bye
Does he want the moon to play with*
The stars to run away with
They'll come if you don't cry.

John
In her daddy's arms she's weeping.

Rhiannon
Soon she'll be a sleeping.

John
So close those pretty eyes.

Both
With a lu la lu la lu la lu la
Bye.

Ailsa * She's a beauty Doe.

Dora Crocodile tears. She could sing 'Ten Green Bottles', they'd be rolling down her cheeks.

Ailsa Still they break your heart.

Dora John's always had a soft spot for Rhiannon.

Ailsa God, I wish I was young. If I was young now I'd know what to do with it.

Dora Would you have it different?

Ailsa I'd have it better.

Ailsa's voice rises high.

Once a native maiden and a stranger met
Underneath a blue Tahitian moon.
The stars were in her eyes
Gardenias in her hair*
And she vowed to care for ever.

Ailsa's singing fades into the distance. The waves are loud.

Martin * There's someone watching.

Rena Shite.

Martin Rena!

Rena runs along the beach.

Rena Noelle hey!

Noelle Hay's for horses.

Martin Rena!

Noelle Who's your friend?

Rena Why are you always so far behind?

They walk up the beach to the cove.

Noelle Pleasure.

Rena Eh?

Noelle Rush at a thing, Rena, and it's over before it's begun. Who's he?

Rena A friend.

Noelle Sneaky.

Rena How am I?

Noelle I like the look of him.

Ailsa's singing drowns out the sound of the waves.

Ailsa
    Then one lonely day the stranger sailed away
    With a parting kiss that came too soon*
    And now the Trade Winds sigh
    As ships go sailing by
    Underneath a blue Tahitian moon.

David * Back to back. Come on now. / Noelle. I'm talking to you. Come on Rena.

John We'll tell you who the tallest is but for the bonniest we'll leave you to fight it out between you. As for the sweetest natured we'll leave that for the future to decide. I've never met a sweet natured woman yet. Not after I've married one.

Ailsa Been married often then have you?

John There's married and married.*

Ailsa What's that supposed to mean?

Dora * That's enough John.*

Ailsa I don't need you to fight my battles Dora.

Noelle * I'm tallest see. Don't have to / stand back to back to tell that.

Ailsa   I may not be the first woman in your life John Williams. But I'll make damn sure I'm the last.

John   Is that a threat?

Ailsa   It's a promise.

John   Don't I have a say?

Ailsa   You had your say when you married me. You've said a couple of things since that haven't been so hot but I'm prepared to overlook them.

John   Here, Noelle. Here's a fried egg roll. Of my making, mind. Nice and hot and fresh out the pan. One for you Rena. Now. My advice to you. Take yourselves away. Don't let your sweet young selves be contaminated by this witch I married. Gareth don't you marry. Don't you ever marry.

He sings. David's guitar picks him up.

John
   Oh I've got those mean mean woman blues
   I've got those mean woman blues
   She treats me so bad
   I've got nothing left to lose
   I work* hard to keep her
   But she throws my care away.

The guitar keeps the twelve bar going.

Ailsa   * I work, I might paint my nails red but I work my fingers to the bone. You show me a smarter woman when I leave the house in the morning. There isn't a smarter woman in our street. Nor any house with cleaner windows.* My windows shine. My baking tins are aye filled with gypsy creams and Empire biscuits. My stovies are unrivalled. You're living with a miracle John Williams. You're living with a miracle and you don't even know it.

John
> * Oh I work so hard to keep her
> But she throws my care away
> The Lord will judge me willin'
> When I come to him on judgement day.

Ailsa Tell me you don't love me John Williams. Tell me that and I'll leave this cove and I'll leave this beach and I'll take my daughter and you'll never have truck with either one of us again. My God, sometimes I wish you would tell me. Tell me before I lose my looks John. Do me that favour. Then I can go out and I can find someone that'll appreciate me.

Dora You'll never learn will you.

Ailsa What the hell does that mean?

Dora There was the wicked one and there was the good one. You got the wicked one.

Ailsa And you got what you deserved isn't that right Dora?

John sings.

John
> * Oh I've got those mean mean woman blues . . .

The guitar takes over. Another joins in and another. The girls slush through a shallow stream flowing over stones.

Rena * Jesus this is freezing.

Noelle Fresh water's colder than the sea of course.

Rena You know everything I suppose.

Noelle You have no idea.

Rena Don't start.

Noelle   What?

Rena   Just don't start, right.

They wade through the stream. Rocks shift in the shallow water.

Noelle   Your Da makes great egg rolls.

Rena   D'you want mine?

Noelle   Don't you?

Rena   You can have it.

Noelle   Thank you.

Rena   Want a mud bath?

Noelle   What do you mean?

Rena   Lie down and I'll cover you with mud and it'll bake hard in the sun and it'll paralyse you.

Noelle   I'm eating an egg roll amn't I.

Rena   I'll start with your feet.

Noelle   Go on then.

She sits down with a splash.

Rena   Your skin's very dark.

Noelle   Jesus, he makes them salty.

Rena   Take a drink. You could bottle and sell it, this water. See, Welsh water. I love it when I come here.

Noelle   You never invite us up there.

Rena   My dad would live down here if he could. He's happy here that's what he says.

Noelle   Is that happiness? When I'm happy I hope I never look like he does.

The sound of mud slapping.

Ow Rena. Watch it.

Rena   Hold still then.

The mud slaps and slaps.

What're you staring at?

Noelle   You've got thin thighs. I wish I had thin thighs. I'm going to take after my mother. These are my best years. Depresses me sometimes. Why do you have to spend longer old than you do young?

Rena   Your waist's quite small.

Noelle   Do you think a man could get his hands round it?

Rena   Depends how big his hands are.

Noelle   I long for the feel of a man's hands at my waist. I want to feel small in his hands. Like a wild and delicate flower.

Rena   You've got yellow douk running down your chin.

Noelle   Tickles.

Rena   It's not very attractive.

Noelle   Some man might find it so. I might be sitting at breakfast with my husband one morning. And my breakfast egg will spurt and he'll come round the breakfast table, my husband will, and he'll lick the running egg from off my chin.

Rena   That's horrible.

Noelle   Only if you're Scottish.

Rena   A man licking your chin?

Noelle The whole Scottish nation suffers from guilt and prudishness.

Rena Says who?

Noelle You want to remember you're your father's daughter.

Rena What does that mean?

Noelle He's licked some chins in his time.

Rena Whose chin?

Noelle Feel how hard this mud is. That sun's baking.

Rena What d'you mean about my dad, Noelle?

Pause. A bird cries.

Noelle The heat in this mud. I feel all lackadaisical. / I do really.

Rena You'll feel dead in a minute. You'll get this mud in your mouth and you'll suffocate, Noelle Williams.

Noelle Are you going to put it there?

Rena Don't tempt me.

Noelle You think you can take me on?

Rena I know I can.

Noelle I'll tell you about your father. I wasn't going to because I'm fond of you Rena and I'm not a cruel person. But you force my hand. You've got mud in my hair.

Rena Jesus, Noelle.

Noelle Blasphemy's common Rena. That's your mother's colours slipping through there. If you're very lucky your Welsh side might save you.

Rena You are such a bitch.

Noelle I've had yearly lessons, Rena Williams.

Rena Are you going to tell me about my father or are you not?

Beat.

Noelle I'm not. Not yet anyway.

Rena gets up and runs away along the bed of the stream. Noelle calls after her.

Careful Rena. Rena. You'll break your bloody leg.*
Come and get this mud off me. Rena. Rena.

Her voice fades into the sound of rushing water and Rena's panting.

Rena (*whispers*) * Dear Mr Manning. Dear, dear, dear Mr Manning. I've a candidate for murder I want to introduce you to. I've got your number nine sitting in a fresh water stream in Wales waiting to have your knife plunge into her guts. Dear Mr Manning please don't take any other applications. This is important. Noelle Williams is the one for you. Please get yourself down here by the quickest method of travel. I'll reimburse any expenses you incur though it might take me a while. Girls can be bad bitches Mr Manning but Noelle Williams takes the biscuit. She'll make an awful woman when she comes to maturity. You'd be doing the world a favour were you to cease her being. About dinner time should suit. We'll all be gathered. You'll know the bitch by her yellow swimsuit and the rolls of fat on her upper arms. And the three necklace of Venus lines that circle her dark neck. She says they're a promise of the beauty that is to come. Don't go confusing the two of us. There's some maintain we look alike. I have no necklace of Venus round my neck as Noelle kindly pointed out

last year. I have a red swimsuit, Mr Manning. Just so
you know. It clashes with my hair but my mother says
be brazen and be damned. She bought me the swimsuit.
If only you were God Mr Manning. If you were God
I would ask you to let me sing so that I could join them.
I'm all alone here Mr Manning. My Father would
forgive me the guitar if I could sing. Noelle can sing.
And Rhiannon. I can hear it. I dream it, Mr Manning.
I dream it so hard that when I wake up I can taste it.
My own voice and it's lovely. Then I open up my mouth.
And the sound that I hear. Mr Manning, it's an abomi-
nation. And it hurts my heart. Kill Noelle for me please.
She only has to look at me. She knows all my misery.
She knows it better than I do myself. That's not a thing
any person should have to suffer. So you just kill her.
We're all here on earth for a purpose. Your purpose is
to rid the world of Noelle Williams and make me happy.
No one's all bad Mr Manning. You do this death for me.
It'll be your good deed. It'll get you into Heaven.

Martin   Who are you talking to?

A clink of flint on flint.

Ow.

Rena   Don't you ever spy on me.

Martin   Don't throw stones.

Rena   Tit / for tat.

Martin   You / drew blood.

Rena   You stoned me. / So I stoned you.

Martin   Bloody sharp.

Rena   Not sharp enough.

Martin   You're sick.

Rena   You a wee skink are you, spying on me.

Martin You're a cry baby.

Rena Aye but you want to lick the tears from off my cheeks eh? Otherwise what are you doing hovering around eh?

The sound of the sea. The cry of a bird. The distant desultory strumming of a guitar.

Martin Who's Manning?

Rena What?

Martin 'Dear Mr Manning.' You talking to God?

Rena Since when was God's name Manning? Don't you know anything where you come from?

Martin We learn quickly. Who's Manning?

Rena He's murdered eight folk so far. Everyone's waiting for number nine. My mum lives in terror. See, when the curtains are shut she thinks she hears him climbing up the rhone pipes. I hide under the kitchen table.

Martin From Manning?

Rena In the afternoon. When the cakes come out and the women talk. 'Manning' they say like they love him. Jesus they talk about nothing else.

Martin Why don't the police arrest him?

Rena See. What it is. The police know it's him. They trail him the whole time. They even drink with him in the club that he goes to. But they've got no evidence. He knows it and they know it. They have to wait for him to slip up. So far he hasn't. It's quite exciting. Used to be they scared you with the bogey man if you were bad. You know? Now it's Manning. 'Eat your mince or Manning'll get you.'

43

Martin   We could swim.

Rena   So we could.

Martin   Will we?*

Rena   What?

Martin   Swim.

Rena   If you like.

In the cove.

John   * Come on Doe. This is your song.

Three chords.

Dora
As I sailed my ship across the water
When to Hawaii I said good bye
All the world seemed sad and still as if
It saw my grief and heard my cry.

Ailsa's soprano comes in in harmony.

Both
Farewell to thee.

The guitar breaks off.

John   I always preferred the single voice on that song.

Gareth   I'll help myself to black pudding will I?

John   Give me a contralto for a contralto sends shivers up and down my spine.

Ailsa   Maybe you should have married one.

John   Missed my chance didn't I?

Gareth   I'll help myself then. Da?

David   You're on your own son.

John 'Farewell to thee' Doe-Doe.

Three chords.

Dora
> Farewell to thee
> Farewell to thee
> My passion flower for whom I long in vain*
> One fond farewell
> And faithful we will be
> Until we meet again
> Farewell.

Waves break on the stones at the sea's edge. The singing's far off.

Martin * Right so. What you have to do. You have to stand with the water up to your neck. And you have to keep quite still and let the waves go right over your head.

Rena How do you breath?

Martin It's all in the timing.

Rena I'm not allowed out of my depth.

Martin In England we always do this.

Rena You must think I'm awful thick.

Martin No.

She imitates him.

Rena 'No.' Why can't you talk right? Say 'no'.

He imitates her.

Martin 'No.'

Rena Why can't you talk like that all the time?

Martin   You don't have to do the wave thing if it frightens you.

Rena   I'm not frightened of the sea. There's only one thing I'm frightened of.

Martin   What's that?

Rena   I'm not quite sure. But I'll tell you this by the way. Her up there, the hippopotamus in the mud. Noelle. She's going to make damn sure I find out. What did I ever do to her Martin? You answer me that. For I must have done something. She hates me Martin. So she does.

Martin   Hate's a big word.

Rena   Popacatapetl that's a big word. Hate's easy learned.

Martin   Where are you going?

Rena   To the waves. Come on.

The waves break and break. The reflection of the sunlight blinds up from the water.

Blackout.

End of Act One.

Act Two

The heat shimmers on the horizon. It's almost audible in the grass cove.

Ailsa For God's sake keep still Rhiannon.

Rhiannon It's fidget time of day. Look see. Dad and Gareth are wandering. There's Mum and Uncle John on the cliff path.

Ailsa Is there someone else up there?

Rhiannon Why do you quarrel?

Ailsa Your eyes are aye on that clifftop.

Rhiannon Lying in bed when I was little, I used to listen to you all. The sound of the guitars floating up to my bedroom late at night. Made me feel safe.

Ailsa Other days.

Rhiannon I liked them.

Ailsa Have you got St Vitus dance?

Rhiannon It's hot that's all.

Ailsa Go for a swim.

Rhiannon Plenty time for that.

Ailsa Who the hell are you looking for?

  Pause.

You must think I'm in my dotage.

Rhiannon I'm not looking for anyone.

Ailsa   Have it your own way. Looking up there with your 'come to bed' eyes.

She sings at Rhiannon.

Embrace me
My sweet embraceable you.

Don't tell me Rhiannon. I wasn't born yesterday.

Embrace me
You irreplaceable you
Just one look at you my heart grew tipsy in me.

We've all been there.

Rhiannon   I don't know what you're talking about.

Ailsa
Just one look at you brings out the gypsy in me.

Is he nice?

Rhiannon   You have a vivid imagination Auntie Ailsa.

Ailsa   Don't come it Rhiannon. Don't you come it.

She lies back in the sun, still singing the Gershwin song. But to herself now. And it becomes about John. And there are tears in her eyes.

I love all the many charms about you
Above all I want my arms about you
Don't be a naughty baby
Come to Mama, come to Mama do
My sweet embraceable you.

The wind soughs through the long dry grass by the side of the cliff path.

John   Come on into the long grass Dora.

Dora   What for?

John Privacy.

Dora No touching.

John I'm offering you my hand so you don't fall. I'm offering you my hand, what's wrong with that Dora?

Dora I know you.

John Sit with me in the long grass. Talk to me, that's all.

Dora Where does talk lead?

John Wherever you want it to. You're in charge Dora.

Dora Promise to be good John.

John Come on. I'll be as good as you want me to be. Come on.

The grass swishes around them.

John There's a hawk.

Dora Take your hand off from round my waist.

John Don't you want to see the hawk.

Dora Where?

John See how still he is.

Dora That's a buzzard John.

John I could drink that sky.

Dora I'd rather drink a milk stout.

John You haven't an ounce of romance in you.

Dora I've been playing this game with you for the last – I've lost count of the years. If that's not romantic I don't know what is.

*John kisses her and for a moment she's as passionate
as he is. Then she breaks away from him.*

Who's there?

John   No one.

Dora   Is it one of the kids?

John   Rabbit maybe.

Dora   I don't want the kids seeing us.

John   There's no one there Dora.

*His fingers tease at the bottom of her dress lifting it so
that his hand's on her thigh.*

Dora   I heard something.

John   You're jittery, that's all.

Music.

*She lets him calm her. Allowing his hands free range.
The music and the heat of the afternoon soothe. Then
she pulls half away.*

Dora   This is daft John. What we're doing.

John   Not doing anything are we? Not even talking.
Not sensible talking. We could sit down Dora. We could
at least do that. Be hidden by the grass then.

They sit.

Dora   Only for a minute.

John   Come here.

Dora   Oh God John. Listen.

John   What? What for God's sake?

Dora   Bach.

John Bach?

Dora David's playing Bach John. He's not happy.

John Where're you going?

Dora To his side.

John What about me?

Dora I'm thirteen stone and ten pounds John and my husband's playing Bach. Let me go.

John What's your weight got to do with it?

Dora There was a time once when I would have lain on a bed of nails with you and thought myself lucky. I'd have looked at the sky till my neck broke. Now heart, listen to me. It would be awful if we were found out now, you and me, when my passion's fulfilled by a hymn with the choir, a sit in a pub and a long cool glass by my hand.

John Stay with me until I go and cook the curry. That's all. Let him play Bach. He's not out looking for us if he's doing that.

He takes her in his arms.

Dora We're old for kisses.

John No such thing.

Dora I'm fat.

John You're like a river salmon.

She laughs.

Lush.

She doesn't leave him. She lets him coax her down into the grass.

Noelle's looking down on John's hollow from the top of the cliff.

Wind in the grass. A sharp scream.

Man Spying are you?

Noelle Get your hands off me.

Man If you can see them they can see you.

Noelle They're too busy to be looking up here to the cliff top.

Man I don't like spies.

Noelle's startled but defiant.

Noelle Your likes and dislikes mean nothing to me.

Man That your Mammy?

Noelle Everyone's Scottish today.

Man You're not.

Noelle Thank God for that.

Man Eh?

Noelle What I know of your lot I don't like.

Man My my my.

Noelle Who the hell are you?

Man Go swim with your friends.

Noelle They're no friends of mine.

Man Your mammy's talking.

Noelle Is that what you call it?

Man You leave her to talk.

Noelle Why should I?

Man Spying's the act of a mean person.

Noelle That's Rena Maeve Williams' father and he's holding my mother in his arms. Am I supposed to put up with that?

Man They're not doing you any harm.

Noelle I know exactly who you are. I could blow the whistle on you if I had half a mind.

Man Go on with you. Go away.

Noelle That's changed your tune.

Man Go. Go, go, go.

Noelle Make me.

Man Yaaaaaaaaa.

Noelle gasps in fright and runs. The man laughs. It's not an unpleasant laugh. Not at all. Noelle yells from afar.

Noelle Are you not ashamed of yourself?

Man I'm not if you're not.

Noelle You frightened me.

Man You're easy frightened then.

Noelle I'll tell on you.

The man's teasing laughter accompanies her running feet. Wind and sea and the cry of a bird. The sound of breaking waves. The water ripples around Martin and Rena. Loud panting.

Rena My God. My God.

Martin Another one coming.

Rena screams. The scream's muffled by water.

Heartbeats and the odd not quite silence of the underwater world.

Beyond the surface. Wind and sea and the cry of a bird.

Rena and Martin break the surface. Heave breath into their lungs.

Martin What did you see? What did you see down there?

Rena Jesus, I'm dying.

Martin What did you see?

Rena What did you see?

Martin Took the heart out of me.

Rena Was it Manning?

Martin It was the devil. It was the devil coming in his chariot.

Rena It was Manning. He heard my call. He's down in the depths come all the way from Glasgow. She better watch out Martin. Noelle. I've summoned him, Martin. Manning's nearly here. And if you're good to me Martin. I'll let you ask for a death too. Whose would you ask for Martin?

Beat.

Martin Wave coming.

Rena How long till you die for want of breath?

Martin I don't know.

Rena Are you scared?

Martin Wave coming now.

Heartbeats fading into Rhiannon and Ailsa chopping vegetables on wooden chopping boards in the cove.

Rhiannon   Can I ask you something Auntie Ailsa?

Ailsa   Ask away. Asking's free. Do some more carrots.

Rhiannon   Am I my father's daughter?

Ailsa   Oh good. A riddle. I like riddles.

Rhiannon   If I had a child I'd like her to know who her grandfather was.

Ailsa   Are you expecting?

The sound of chopping fades into the sound of the waves.

Rena   God I'm freezing.

Martin   Want a towel?

Rena   Eh?

Martin   I'll get you one.

He runs over the stones. Rena calls after him.

Rena   Martin!

His footsteps fade into the sound of chopping in the cove.

Rhiannon   You know who my father is. Why shouldn't I?

Ailsa   The shock, Rhiannon, and me with a knife in my hand. You take my breath away. So you do.

Rhiannon   Who's my father?

Ailsa   David.

Rhiannon   It's between two people Auntie Ailsa. My mother's husband and yours.

Ailsa   Never mind the celery. Go and swim. Go on, go on. Give me the knife.

Rhiannon   I'm asking you a question.

Pause.

Ailsa   That's my knife. Give it to me.

Beat.

Your mother would cry to hear you. And David. My God what would he do? Go and swim. Go on. I don't need you here. I don't want you. You're too thin and you're too young and you're bothering me. Give me my knife Rhiannon.

The Bach floods into the sound of the bubbling cold spring.

Noelle's in the stream splashing Rena. Noelle's laughing. Rena's shivering.

Rena   Stop it, / Noelle. Stop it.

Noelle   Only a bit of fun. / Where's your sense of humour.

Rena   I don't like being splashed. I don't think it's funny.

Noelle   Only being friendly.

Rena   People always say that when they hurt you.

A giggle and a splash.

I'm warning you Noelle.

Noelle   Get your knight errant.

She shouts.

Martin. / Martin. He'll save you.

Rena   Stop it.

She lobs a quick flint.

Noelle   Ow. No call for stones.

Rena   Don't say you weren't warned.

Beat.

Noelle   Your Mum had a son when she had you. But he died. Deformed he was.

Beat.

Rena   We could damn the stream. What about that?

She wades through the water grabbing rocks and heaving them down in a pile.

Noelle   Deformed horribly my mum says. I know you're listening.

Rena   See we could change the way the water runs. We could change it utterly.

A large stone clunks down on the rocky bed of the stream.

Noelle   The softest whimper he gave. Your brother. And then he died in Uncle John's arms. They went into mourning, your mum and dad. No one celebrated when you were born and your father mourns still. Because a girl can't carry on his name. So it's my brother that'll be the head of the family when your dad and my dad are dead and that means something, my mum says. If your dad died here on holiday you wouldn't even get to go to his funeral for women mean that.

She clicks her fingers.

And girls mean less, my Mum says.

Rena   I'll keep his name.

Noelle   Well you can't so.

Rena   I can do anything I want.

Noelle   No woman can. Prisoners of their bodies women are.

Rena   Not me.

Noelle   Your mother can do anything I suppose.

Rena   Course she can.

Noelle   She can't get her husband to love her. She's stupid and you're stupid. You can't play the guitar and you can't sing. You've disappointed your father all the way down the line.

Rena   There was no twin brother.

Noelle   When have I ever lied to you?

Rena   My father loves me.

Noelle   Love's conditional Rena. It always was and it always will be.

Rena   I'll never take any other man's name but my father's.

Noelle   Your husband won't like that.

Rena   He'll have to take me as he finds me. He can have my body but he can't have my name and that's that. And if he doesn't like it I'll find one that does.

Noelle   You think a lot of yourself.

Rena   If I don't who will?

Noelle   A man doesn't like that in a woman. A man likes a woman to be modest in her endeavours and her achievements and to show a proper respect. See your attitude. Your attitude's the trowel that you'll dig your own slow grave with. You'll die alone Rena Maeve Williams. You mustn't be too powerful. Not obviously anyway. You must be subtle and devious. Dodge and weave, then you'll get your own way. Above all you must be clever.

Rena   I'll keep my father's name. That's my colour. I was born with it. I'll keep it for his sake and for my brother's sake that died though I didn't know it till this moment. I'll learn to play the guitar and when my father dies I'll play it in his stead every Hogmanay and the whiskies will build up under my chair as they do now under his. And I'll keep going till the morning light and I'll sing the old songs in my father's memory. I've got music in my soul. One day I'll find a way to let it out. When I do my father'll look down from on high with my baby brother on his lap and he'll love me very much and be proud of me for what I've become.

Noelle   It won't be legal.

Rena   Eh?

Noelle   You'll bear a pretend name. And he'll look down from on high with your baby brother on his lap and he'll say to your baby brother. 'She should have died, not you. For her name is a sham and she can't play the guitar to save herself and she's got a voice that slides between the frets and defies all keys and she's an abomination on the face of the earth and that's my Gibson Kalamazoo she's holding that should have gone to my son and heir and her fingers defile it that should never have touched it in the first place for they should be dead fingers and my Gibson Kalamazoo that a dealer offered me real money for and I said 'No,' should be in the hands of my living son and then I'd look down from up here and I'd be happy indeed.'

There's a sob in Rena's voice but it bites.

Rena You've still got yellow douk running down
your chin. It's dried and it's cracked. It's not the most
attractive sight I've ever seen. Don't ever let a man see
you like that Noelle, for you'll turn his stomach and then
where will you be. I can stand on my own two feet. I can
now and I always will. You're a clinging vine Noelle.
You'll die on your own.

The sound of feet running away.

Noelle Rena.

*Noelle picks up water in her hands. Splashes her face
with it. A private voice.*

Noelle You never get food on your chin do you Rena.
One day I'll be as old as my Mother and then I won't
know which chin I've got food on.

*The sound of the stream fades. A knife chops on the
wooden board.*

Ailsa Your eyes are aye straying to that hilltop.

Rhiannon Mind your own business Auntie Ailsa.

Ailsa It's alright for you to satisfy your curiosity is it?
That's alright. But I can't ask a civil question in return.
One brother or the other what difference does it make?

Desultory chopping.

Race you.

Rhiannon What?

The knife's still again.

Ailsa Onion. Catch.

The thud of an onion on the ground.

Butterfingers.

Rhiannon   I've a knife in my hand for God's sake.

Ailsa   Two onions each. First one to finish wins.

Rhiannon   These knives are sharp.

Ailsa   You win, I'll tell you all I know.

Rhiannon   You can't make a game of it.

Ailsa   Why the hell not?

Beat.

Take it or leave it.

Beat.

Go.

Ailsa's knife rapidly chews up an onion on her chopping board.

Rhiannon   I wasn't ready.

Ailsa   You have to be ready for anything in this life Rhiannon. Don't you know that by now. If I hadn't been ready. What I've had to put up with would have sucked the life out of me. But here I am. And here I'll stay. I'm battling against existence Rhiannon. And I'm winning Rhiannon. I'm battling against existence and I'm winning so far.

The chopping's furious and then it fades. The waves are sluggish now. Pulling at the stones. There's a footfall. Noelle gasps in fright.

Martin   What are you doing?

Noelle   Sun bathing.

Martin   You were spying on Rena's mother.

Noelle   You gave me a heart attack.

Martin I beg your pardon.

Noelle Creeping around.

Martin Sorry. I frightened you.

Noelle I'm frightened of nothing.

Martin Where's she gone?

Noelle Who's she? The cat's mother?

Martin Rena.

Noelle You like her, don't you?

Martin I brought her a towel.

Noelle Give it to me.

Martin I brought it for her.

Noelle I'm wet aren't I?

Martin I don't know you.

Noelle You know her do you?

Martin Rena?

Noelle She's an evil cow.

Martin What does that mean?

Noelle Means she's my cousin. She's got red hair and green eyes and everybody turns their heads to look at her when she walks by. That's fine most of the time. Now and then it gets to me. Have I got the yellow off my chin?

Martin I'm not that fond of red hair myself.

Noelle You don't have to say that.

Martin You're very pretty.

Noelle You're a typical Englishman.

Martin What's that mean?

Noelle You've a smooth tongue and you can't be trusted.

Martin You can have the towel.

Noelle I only want to borrow it.

Martin I didn't mean to keep.

The sound of the sea.

Noelle Are you rich?

Martin Why?

Noelle You must be quite well-off.

Martin How?

Noelle We don't have towels like this to waste on the beach. That your Mum?

Martin Uh huh.

Noelle That your brother?

Martin What if it is?

Noelle He's big to be carried.

Martin Is he?

Noelle You look angry.

Martin I'm never angry.

Noelle I get so angry I could kill sometimes. You look angry watching your brother.

Martin I love George.

Noelle Funny that.

Martin What?

Noelle The look on your face doesn't spell out love to me.

Martin What're you shivering for?

Noelle I think you're quite a frightening person. Thank you for the loan of the towel.

Martin We could find Rena.

Noelle I was born on Christmas Day. They call me Noelle.

Martin I know.

Noelle Do we have to find Rena?

Martin She's wild isn't she?

Noelle I think she's common myself but you can call it wild if you like. People don't usually like their names. I like mine very much.

Martin Come on Noelle.

Noelle Sounds especially nice when you say it.

Just one pair of feet run up the beach slithering on the chuckies. Noelle stays where she is. Martin yells back.

Martin Come on.

Noelle walks slowly up the beach.

Noelle!

Noelle Keep your bloody hair on. I'm coming, look. See. I'm coming en't I.

The pebbles crunch and fade into two knives chopping furiously. One knife stops.

Rhiannon I've won.

Ailsa Have you?

Rhiannon You tell me what I want to know.

Ailsa This is the only dish my husband cooks. Every summer of your young life you've had Curry in a Bucket off him. Be honest with me Rhiannon. I know you want to beat me. Can you call to mind a lumpy onion in any one of the curries within your living memory? You can't, can you? Finely chopped they've been and this is the hand that chopped them.

Rhiannon Know what made me question it, who my father was? It was you, Auntie Ailsa. The look in your eye. The way you watched Uncle John when he looked at me. We made a triangle him and you and me.

Ailsa Nonsense.

Rhiannon You're dead scared I'm going to win.

Ailsa Are you chopping? Are you?

Rhiannon I'm chopping. I'm chopping alright.

Frantic chopping on two boards. A caught breath. Then a scream.

Ailsa What is it? / What's wrong? What's the matter.

Rhiannon I've cut the top of my finger off.

Ailsa Don't be / ridiculous.

Rhiannon I have, / I have.

Ailsa Where is / it then?

Rhiannon Auntie Ailsa! / Auntie Ailsa!

Ailsa If you'd cut the top off your finger it would be on your chopping board. Look in the onion. Look in the onion Rhiannon. Do you see a finger? Because I / most certainly do not.

Rhiannon Auntie Ailsa.

Ailsa You were always a tragedy queen Rhiannon. Show me what you've done.

A hiss of breath between teeth.

I'm not saying it's not nasty but you can dry your tears. At least it's all there. Hold your arm up for God's sake. Keep the blood off the onion. I've elastoplast in the picnic bag. Winning isn't everything Rhiannon. You should have been more careful.

The chords for Cole Porter's 'Miss Otis' from afar.

Rhiannon Listen. David plays the sweetest guitar in the world but you wouldn't want to listen to him. Uncle John makes mistakes but you listen and you watch and you just love him.* Everybody does. Don't they Auntie Ailsa?

Ailsa Keep that hand up. I don't want you bleeding to death.

An easy bluesy strum. David's soft sweet tones.

David
　 * When she woke up and found
　 That her dream of love was gone Madame
　 She ran to the man
　 Who had led her so far astray*
　 And from under her velvet gown
　 She drew a gun and shot her lover down
　 Madame, Miss Otis regrets she's unable to lunch today.

The wind rustles the dry grass. A far bird calls.
A private voice.

Rena * Dear Mr Manning. Mr Manning where are you? Mr Manning I can see them all from this cliff top. I'm like a bird up here in the wind and the air. I'm higher than the birds for they're all below me. I'm right on the very edge and I'm very nearly dizzy but I'm not quite. It's better than the waves Mr Manning. I'm battling against myself to stay on this cliff edge. Not to step forward and not to step back. That's my battle. My heart's beating Mr Manning. Can you hear it? I'm more excited than I've ever been in my life. This is the best moment I've had so far. Ever. Ever. Ever. Now I can sing. Now, now, now.

Hands grab Rena. She screams.

Man   Get away / from the edge.

Rena   I knew you'd come.

Man   Care / ful.

Rena   Manning?

Man   You'll fall.

Rena   I will not.

Man   The cliff could crumble.

Rena   I had taken that into consideration.

Man   Had you now?

Rena   Don't patronise me.

Man   I beg your pardon.

Rena   Get your hands off.

Man   Right you are.

Rena   You are him aren't you?

Man   Who are you?

Rena   Rena Maeve Williams.

Man   Pretty name.

Rena   I know you.

Man   Is that a fact?

Rena You come from near where my Gran lives.

Man Where's that then?

Rena Balvicar Street.

Man Nice view of the park.

Rena You do though, don't you?

Man If you say so.

Rena I never forget a face.

Man There's a club I like down there.

Rena I called you.

Man Gonnie get Rhiannon for me?

Rena It's her sister I called you for.

Man She's o'er young for me.

Rena But you must. You must do it.

Man Do what?

Rena Noelle. She's going to tell me something that I don't know. And once she's told me I'll know it. And I'll not be able to unknow it. And my whole life'll change. I don't want that. You've got to stop her. Please Mister. Please, please.

Man How am I to stop her?

Beat.

Rena See her. See her way down there. Noelle's a bitch you know.

Man She looks alright to me.

Rena She's very far away. You wait till you see her up close.

Man I'll take your word for it.

Rena That's my Dad in the grass with my Auntie Doe. He's in love with her. He always has been. See her voice now. That's what he loves. You've only got to have the one beauty. It's supposed to be a secret. Their love. We all know. Doesn't make things too easy between Noelle and me. See. She blames my Dad. And I blame her Mum. And neither of us says what we mean.

Beat.

Don't you think Noelle's just the swankiest awfullest name?

Man Who's the boy?

Rena Martin. I like him.

Man What's your Mother doing?

Rena God knows. She tells a lot, Noelle. But she always knows more than she tells. Feel my heart. I'll die it's beating so fast. You've got to shut her up. You are Manning aren't you? You've got to be him.

In the cove the primus roars. A kettle boils.

Ailsa Hot and sweet for shock.

Rhiannon I don't like it sweet.

Ailsa You'll drink it whether you like it or not.

Rhiannon You're a bully Auntie Ailsa.

Ailsa It's not my fault you know.

Rhiannon What?

Beat.

Ailsa You hope that you're not going to be alone. That's what I hope anyway. Circumstances are such that I find myself to be . . .

Rhiannon My mother loves my father.

Ailsa She should tell my husband that.

Rhiannon Whose child am I?

Ailsa The bleeding's stopped.

Rhiannon Please Auntie Ailsa. Please.

Beat.

Ailsa Will we play another round, Rhiannon? I'll give you another chance.

Rhiannon What?

Ailsa How do you keep that body in trim?

Rhiannon What?

Ailsa It's not absolutely natural. The way you look. Show me what you do to help it.

Rhiannon I exercise Auntie Ailsa, that's all.

Ailsa Teach me the exercises.

Beat.

Close your mouth Rhiannon. Nobody looks quite the thing with their mouth agape be they ever so pretty.

Rhiannon Don't you care at all how I feel?

Ailsa I care about my own child. You've enough people caring about you. If I can do what you do I tell you nothing. If I can't, you get to know what I know. May it do you more good than it has me.

Rhiannon This isn't a game.

Ailsa How come we're all playing it?

Rhiannon You can't do what I do.

Ailsa   You've nothing to lose then.

Rhiannon   I've been dancing all my life Auntie Ailsa.

Ailsa   We've all heard about your dancing Rhiannon.

Rhiannon   You can't just spread your legs and put your head on the sand.

Ailsa   Yes I can. I've been doing Canadian Airforce exercises since the Canadian Airforce came into being. We'll swop. You show me what you do and I'll show you what I do.

Rhiannon   You'll hurt yourself Auntie Ailsa.

Ailsa   I can't hurt more than I do already.

The wind in the long grass. Dora's delighted laughter.

Dora   Don't John. What are you doing?

John   Stopping.

Dora   Not now.

John   'Don't,' you said.

Dora   I've changed my mind.

From the path.

Gareth   Oh my God.

David   Move. Move, move, move.

Gareth   Dad!

He pulls his son round the corner.

David   She see you?

Gareth   No.

David   Sure?

Gareth   Dad, for God's sake.

David Did she see you?

Gareth She didn't see me. / She didn't see me. Alright?

David Come on son.

Gareth You're not even shocked.

David We're walking / aren't we?

Gareth What's going on?

David With you or without you, Gareth.

He walks away.

Gareth Dad.

The wind blows in the hollow. Dora laughs.

John Say you've missed me.

Dora Don't stop.

John Say it.

Dora John.

John Not till you say it.

Dora I've missed you. I've missed you. God damn you John. How could I not?

A bird screams.

Gareth What are you going to do?

David I'm doing nothing.

Gareth Jesus Christ, Dad.

David We don't know. / We didn't see.

Gareth That's your wife.

David If they'd wanted us to see they'd have done it in front of us. Now let it be.

Gareth   Do something. Do anything.

David   I'm walking up this path Gareth. I'm looking down at the ocean. I'm watching the waves break on the shore. And I'm asking you to walk with me.

Wind. A bird cry.

Smoke?

David flicks open a cigarette case. He dunts a cigarette on the metal. Lights Gareth's cigarette and his own. Drags deeply.

Gareth   How long's it been going on?

David   I'd add this to the marriage vows. Keep your secrets. Never breathe. Never hint. Don't tell at the moment of a parting or on the day of a death. Don't let a fight pull it out of you. If you sin. It's your sin. Never cast your sin on another for their forgiveness and your relief. Bear your guilt yourself forever. Confession only injures the hearer. Lock it up. Lock it all inside you. See that? That back there. Who's to say that's not my fault? If that's what your mother needs to give me fifty weeks of her year. So be it. I don't want her to tell me about it. Don't want that ever. The day she tells me's the day I lose her. The longer the time that passes and her silent the more sure I am that she'll never speak. That I'll keep her.

Gareth   You can't live with this.

David   I can. I have.

Gareth   I don't have to.

David   You speak and I'll have nothing left. You've your own life Gareth. This is mine.

Gareth   Where are you going?

David   Going on up. Feel the wind. Coming? Gareth?

Rhiannon counting in the cove. The grass creeps with heat. A bird cries. A small groan.

Rhiannon Two, three, four, five, six, seven, eight.

Ailsa That's a split isn't it? That's a split Rhiannon.

Rhiannon Box split.

Ailsa You didn't bloody think I could. Admit it. Come on.

Rhiannon I didn't think you could.

Ailsa Well I can. I bloody can. What now?

Rhiannon Lay your upper body flat on the ground.

Ailsa What?

Rhiannon Arms out. Bust on the sand.

Ailsa Still in a split?

Rhiannon Don't do it if you feel any strain.

Ailsa There's bound to be some strain isn't there?

Rhiannon Take it slowly.

Ailsa My God it's not possible.

Rhiannon Watch. Five, six, seven, eight.

A slight exhalation of breath.

Ailsa You're allowed to turn your face sideways are you.

Rhiannon Cheek on the sand.

Ailsa Not nose?

Rhiannon Your nose is bigger than mine. Auntie Ailsa. You wouldn't have as far to go.

Ailsa Cheek then. Arms out?

Rhiannon Oh God, Auntie Ailsa.

Ailsa Nothing to it.*

Rhiannon Wait.

Ailsa * You watch Rhiannon. Just you watch.

Rhiannon Auntie Ailsa please.

Ailsa Just takes concentration. Five, six, seven, eight.

A grunt of effort. An awful sound. The noise of a tendon snapping. The littlest sound from Ailsa.

Ailsa Oh.

Rhiannon Oh God.

Ailsa Oh.

Rhiannon Auntie Ailsa?

Ailsa Rhiannon!

Rhiannon Get up Auntie Ailsa.

Ailsa Oh Rhiannon. I'm an awful fool.

Rhiannon Get up. Get up. Please.

Ailsa A bloody, bloody fool.

She wails.

Looking down from the cliff.

Man Your mother's in trouble.

Rena I don't care.

Man Go on down.

Rena I will not.

Man That's your mother. It's the only one you'll ever have. Now you go on down to her. Or you'll get a skelp from me.

Rena No man lifts his hand to me.

Man I'll count to three.

Rena I thought you'd be different.

Man One.

Rena You're not the least bit what I expected.

Man Two.

Rena You're a hell of a disappointment do you know that?

Man Go on. Go on. Get.

Rena runs down the cliff path past Martin and Noelle.

Martin Look out Rena.

Noelle Be careful.

Martin Where are you going?

Rena Are you deaf?

Noelle It wasn't your Mum screaming?

Rena Uh huh it was.

Noelle Oh Jesus. I'm coming Rena.

Martin Can I come?

Noelle This is family.

The sound of running feet.

Martin I'll see you later. Rena? Noelle?

His voice fades as they run.

I'll see you later won't I?

There's a dry heat in the cove.

Rhiannon They're all coming Auntie Ailsa. Tell me. Tell me quick. Which one of them's my dad?

Ailsa How can I tell you what I don't know?

She sniffs again.

Feel the smell of that curry. Your father's curries. Curry and tears, eh? Curry and tears.

The roar of the primus. The clang of a pail. The scrape of metal on metal.

John Hands off Rhiannon.

Rhiannon I can cook.

John I make the curries.

Rhiannon You want a bit of help don't you?

John No other hand but mine.*

John slaps Rhiannon's hand.

Rhiannon Ow.

John * Be told will you? What age are you?

Rhiannon Old enough to go barefoot in some man's kitchen.

Beat.

John I'm not so easily impressed.

Rhiannon Wasn't trying to impress you.

John What then?

Rhiannon Uncle . . .

John Drop the Uncle, shall we? I'm sure you're old enough for that.

Rhiannon What will I call you?

John I think we'll make do with John, don't you?

Rhiannon I've got a boy-friend then, John.

John Not so very hard to come by for a girl with average looks. Most men have their tongues hanging out. The surprise would be if you didn't have something sniffing at your heels.

Rhiannon Was that supposed to be an insult?

John Oh I can do better than that with insults if I just set my mind to it.

Rhiannon I want to live with him.

John Give me the cloth. I don't want to burn my hand.

John holds the pail steady while he gives the curry a turn with a wooden spoon.

John I gather we're not talking about marriage.

Rhiannon I want my father to wish me luck.

The pail handle scrapes down the side of the pail.

John You want to go off and be some man's whore?

Rhiannon I'm going to London today.

John In your bathing suit?

Rhiannon I took him a case last night.

John You'll break your mother's heart.

Rhiannon I thought my father might comfort her.

John Your father's the man who brought you up. He may be quiet but he cares.

Rhiannon There's a tone in my father's voice that I hate. I hear it in my own voice. For I take after him. There's a light in his eyes that I love, that I'm glad to see in mine. Will you not wish me luck?

Beat.

John That your friend up there?

Rhiannon He's a nice man.

John 'Nice' puts on a suit and walks up to the altar.

Rhiannon He loves me.

John He'll live with you. He'll take what he wants. He'll never marry you. One day you'll have lines around your eyes, Rhiannon. And he'll find someone younger. I'm warning you.

Rhiannon Not all men are like you.

John What kind of bastard do you think I am?

Rhiannon He's already married, John. He married a Pape.

Pause.

John If there's any trouble. I'll come running to you. Conversely. You know where I am. You come to me. And if you're barefoot and pregnant in his kitchen let me know the child you give birth to. Will you do that?

Rhiannon I will always keep in touch with you.

John That's my own girl.

The sound of the waves. Footsteps on stone.

Dora You alright?

Ailsa All the better for seeing you.

Dora Don't start.

Ailsa Och well.

Dora Don't you want us to take you to hospital?

Ailsa It's a torn ligament.

Dora Bad enough.

Ailsa   It's my own damn fault.

Rhiannon's walking up the cliff path.

Dora   Where's Rhiannon going?

Ailsa   You've had your mind on other things, Dora. She's been watching that cliff top all day.

Dora   What for?

Ailsa   That's what for.

Dora   Who is he?

Ailsa   He's a stranger to me Dora. But by her greeting I'd guess Rhiannon knows him well enough.

Dora   She's only a baby.

Ailsa   He doesn't seem to think so.

Dora   What's she playing at?

Ailsa   Go and ask her that yourself.

Dora   I can see me puffing up that cliff. I can just see me.

Ailsa   You should diet, do you know that?

Dora   She's not going Ailsa. She's not leaving. Oh my God. She should come here to me. She should say goodbye to me.

Ailsa   David's there.

Dora   That's my child. She'd never have been born but for me. He can't say as much. She says goodbye to him though. Girls and their fathers. I should have had sons.

Dora starts up the path.

Ailsa   For God's sake Dora you can't run up there. You'll have a heart attack.

Dora 'You want another child find someone else to sire it.' That's what he said after Gareth. David. French letters. My God I hate the things. I thought I could get him lost in passion. Not him. We'd be making love, he'd stop and out they'd come. He never forgot. Not once in the three years between Gareth and Rhiannon. My husband is utterly dependable. My good, good man. I was thin then. All my days went on devising ways to make him lose his head. My God practically acrobatic I was. I hurt with thirst for another child. I made love to his brother. Not that I loved John. Never did. Never have. Don't now. Children I had a passion for. They are the loves of my life.

Ailsa My poor John.

Pause.

I have passion in me that's not been touched yet. I have such a wealth in me. I'll die when all my passion's spent. That's your daughter walking up that path and she didn't say goodbye. I don't blame her. I'd walk away from you if I could.

Dora You should have stopped coming here years ago.

Ailsa It's my fault now is it? For God's sake, Dora, don't cry. If I'm not I don't see why you should.

Dora I've lost my beautiful daughter.

Ailsa She'll be back. Don't you worry. She'll be back bearing a child in her arms that she'll ask you to look after. For God's sake. Stop your greeting. We've two weeks to dig a hole on this beach and bury the past in it. We'll communicate by letter after that. We'll take Rena abroad next year. After all she's my only child. It's high time she saw the advantage of that. Maybe we'll ski at Christmas. We've the Cairngorms on our doorstep. I've a good job. I make the most of the limited talent God's granted me.

Dora   I envy you your work.

Ailsa   Dry your eyes for God's sake. / Reach me a cushion for my leg hurts.

The wind and the grass and the cry of the birds. Rena's private voice.

Rena   Dear Mr Manning. Come down from the roof of the world. Please, please Mr Manning come down here and kill them all.

Noelle's eating curry with a spoon from a china bowl.

Noelle   Who're you talking to?

Rena   The murderer on the cliff top.

Noelle   I met him.

Rena   You can't let me have anything to myself can you? You've always got to stick your nose in.

Noelle   You can have Martin.

Rena   I don't want Martin.

Noelle   Just because he's English.

Rena   I like him. I don't want him.

Noelle   My mother says never marry a Welsh man. They don't know how to pay a compliment.

Rena   What does your mother know about the English?

Noelle   Just because she's fat, Rena Williams, doesn't mean she hasn't travelled.

Rena   He's coming down from the top of that cliff and he's going to murder the whole lot of us.

Noelle   It's Rhiannon's boy-friend.

Rena   Don't talk shite.

Noelle I like knowing things. It's special. I like being special. I'm very good at it. I'll be special all my life.

   A guitar.

This is rare good curry.

Rena I don't like it.

Noelle You depress me do you know that? Give it here.

Rena Look at them, Dora and Ailsa. They could almost be friends they're so close.

Noelle Know what they're talking about?

Rena Shut up.

Noelle My Mum / and your Dad.

Rena Shite.

Noelle You're like an / ostrich you are.

Rena Shite / shite shite.

Noelle Ostrich. Ostrich. Bowl's empty. Go and get me some more curry.

Rena Get it yourself.

Noelle My Mum stuck holes in French letters to get Rhiannon, though she was ashamed of doing it. And when the holes didn't work she got your Dad to do the necessary. Which was quite considerate of her because it kept it all in the family. Do you believe me?

Rena She's very pretty, Rhiannon.

Noelle Say you believe me or I'll tell you something else.

   Pause.

Rena There's no more to tell.

Noelle Is there not?

Rena Is there?

Noelle It's there in front of you. It's there inside you. You only have to reach for it.

Beat.

Easter's a movable feast, Christmas is not. The year I was born Easter was early and your dad came down to Cardiff. Work out the rest yourself. You're too big to be spoon fed.

Rena Where are you going?

Noelle Maybe I'll swim with Martin.

Noelle walks away across the stones.

Rena I like Martin. Noelle. Noelle. We better take the bowls back.

Beat.

You're my sister too are you? Noelle?

Noelle's laughing as she walks down to the sea's edge.

Noelle. Mr Manning. I've got her for life now. You could have prevented this. You only had to lift your hand. Never trust a man. Never trust a woman. Trust your own self that's the only one you can be sure of. I've learnt a lesson this day. You've let me down badly do you know that? Do you hear me Mr Manning? Are you listening to me? Sod you then.

She runs along the beach. Noelle shouts.

Noelle See him. See Rhiannon with him. One day somebody'll kiss me like that. After all I've got breasts.

Rena You can't swim straight after curry.

Noelle   I don't know what's in store for me Rena. I don't know and I don't want to know. But I'm telling you this. Death by drowning isn't it.

A voice begins to sing 'Good Morning Blues'.

Gareth
    I laid down last night
    Turning from side to side*
    I laid down last night
    Turning from side to side
    But I wasn't sick
    Just dissatisfied.

Noelle   * Listen to him. Gareth. Pity your father has no son.

Rena   I'll be good one day. I'll be good at something anyway. Maybe I'll be an engineer. He'd like that, my dad. If I was an engineer the guitar wouldn't matter.*

The waves break. The birds cry.

Gareth
    I woke up this morning
    Blues sneaking round my head
    I woke up this morning
    Blues sneaking round my head
    I couldn't eat
    Blues all in my bread.
    Good morning Blues*
    Blues how do you do?

Other voices quietly join in the song, Ailsa and Dora and John.

Good morning blues
Blues how do you do?
I'm doing alright
Good morning how are you?

David With me Doe Doe. With me now.

Dora
Drifting and dreaming
While shadows fall
Softly at twilight
I hear you call.

The pebbles ebb and flow with the pull of the waves.
Martin shouts.

Martin Rena! Noelle!

Dora's singing in the distance.

Dora
Love's old sweet story
Told with your eyes*
Drifting and dreaming
Sweet Paradise.

The sound of splashing water. Screams and shouts and
laughter. A wave breaks.

Rena * It's a mystery. Jesus.

Noelle What?

Rena Life. Noelle!

Noelle You just tell it to wait right where it is. Life?
I can't wait to get my hands on it.

The waves break and break. The guitar plays on.
There's laughter at the water's edge.

The End.